Corsica

I0639278

Berlitz Publishing Company, Inc.
Princeton   Mexico City   London   Eschborn   Singapore

Text:	Lindsay Bennett
Editor:	Media Content Marketing, Inc.
Photography:	Pete Bennett
Cover Photo:	Pete Bennett
Photo Editor:	Naomi Zinn
Layout:	Media Content Marketing, Inc.
Cartography:	Raffaele De Gennaro

*Although the publisher tries to insure the accuracy of all the infor-
mation in this book, changes are inevitable and errors may result.
The publisher cannot be responsible for any resulting loss, incon-
venience, or injury. If you find an error in this guide, please let the
editors know by writing to Berlitz Publishing Company, 400
Alexander Park, Princeton, NJ 08540-6306.*

ISBN 2-8315-6985-0

Printed in Italy
010/101 NEW

CONTENTS

● A in the text denotes a highly recommended sight

Corsica

CORSICA AND ITS PEOPLE

Corsica is the third largest island in the Mediterranean Sea. It sits 170 km (105 miles) south of France, to which it belongs, and 83 km (51 miles) west of Italy. Its 8,700 sq km (5,000 sq miles) of land offer striking contrasts and a wealth of natural wonders to explore. Citizens of Corsica, proud, independent people, have long yearned for self-determination, but Corsica is the birthplace of France's greatest hero and inspiration Napoléon Bonaparte; thus it is bound through its most famous son to the land across the water.

It is part of France, but not of France, and this adds to its allure. Corsicans refer to France as "the Continent," indicating its difference from their native land. You can certainly find crusty French bread in the *boulangerie*, but the person serving you may speak to colleagues in the Corsican language, still used at home by much of the population.

Tha land itself offers much to be proud of. Nature has bestowed the gift of amazing geographical variety here. With 1,000 km (625 miles) of coastline, there are beaches of fine golden sand, rocky bays where fishing villages cling to sheltered coves, and sheer cliffs dropping dramatically into the azure water below. Inland a spine of vertiginous granite peaks climb to 2,710 m (8,943 ft), giving Corsica the nickname "mountain in the sea." These mountains collect a cap of snow in the winter months; the meltwater feeds over 25 watercourses, ensuring an ample supply of fresh water for plants, animals, and people. The south has soft Miocene chalk cliffs, while the northernmost tip is schist, rock split and folded by immense geological forces. The weather too has played its part; wind has eroded the softer rock into magnificent and grotesque shapes, while frost and snow have softened the sharp fringes of the mountain ranges.

Differences in altitude and soil produce numerous types of vegetation. Swathes of majestic pines blanket the high peaks. To the east chestnut forests form a mantle over the lower slopes, while in the west the olive is king. Wide coastal plains support crops of vegetables and vines. And the low hills are covered with scrubland called *maccia*, which for centuries sheltered star-crossed lovers, pirates, and vagabonds; it fills the Corsican air with the fragrance of herbs and flowers.

The land plays host to many creatures, from the smallest lizards resting in rocky crevices to wild boar (*sanglier*) grubbing up chestnuts, mountain goats (*mouflon*) bounding confidently along the rocky precipices, and the majestic cerf, a large species of deer found grazing in the remote valleys. Shallow salt lakes in the east provide an excellent habitat for native and migrating birds. Eagles and buzzards rule the high mountain passes, while woodpeckers tap at forest bark and myriad swallows swoop over the rooftops of Corsican towns.

The island has been inhabited since prehistoric times; this early population left their mark with burial mounds and ceremonial sites. Though man settled here, he has never tamed this place — its mountains are too numerous, its furthest valleys too remote. When the ancient Greeks settled here in the

Vibrant wildflowers blossom on a coastal clifftop, high above the sea.

Corsicans have always marched to the beat of a different drummer — citizens differ from those in mainland France.

sixth century B.C., they called the island *Kalliste*, the beautiful one. Today the French still call Corsica *Ile de Beauté*, because Corsica is still a beautiful place. Its natural endowments have not been spoiled by overdevelopment; there are acres of wild land to explore; the air is still fresh, and the climate conducive to time spent outdoors.

For centuries, native Corsicans lived in harmony with the land and sea, trusting in God for protection, as the many churches on the island attest. They kept domesticated animals, which they moved to high ground in the summer months to take advantage of the good grazing. The men hunted the indigenous wild animals, or fished from small boats. The women made the most of the glut of fruit and vegetables, preparing meals with whatever was in season and preserving the rest. Clothes were made from wool and leather, and domestic utensils from wood, slate, and stone. The Corsicans even built metal forges on their island. Those who lived in villages high in the hills had to be self-sufficient, as many were difficult to reach; some were cut off completely in the winter months. Those who lived on the coast, particularly in the east, traded with and picked up influences from the outside world, but also held on to most of the old ways.

Although today Corsica is a thoroughly modern island, these ways of life still survive. Corsican self-sufficiency (some may call it indifference to modern development) has protected this place from the excesses and blights found in other island communities. There is still a rural tradition here, where seasons, not the hands of a watch, mark the passing of time.

Most of the village communities here are healthy where in other countries they have been drained of residents, because tourism has not replaced other economic activity — it has simply become another string in the bow. The local phemoneon of the *ferme auberge* (farm restaurant) is an excellent example; in the summer, when the crops are ripening, a farming family will open a small

Corsican men exchange news about the day's catch outside of a boat shop.

restaurant, making meals with their own produce to augment the profits they will make from their crops in the fall. Owners of car or watersports equipment rental franchises may have other, more traditional forms of income as well — this keeps the economy in balance. No towering hotels have been built to blot the landscape; no cheap mementos from elsewhere are imported here, as good quality, home-produced goods are sold in the souvenir shops.

Throughout history, Corsica has been fought over by a series of major European powers — though mostly ruled by Genoa — and evidence of this can be seen at every turn. Magnificent fortresses are at the center of many coastal towns, and over thirty 15th-century watchtowers sit at important vantage points around the coast. Over the centuries, Corsicans learned to fear the coming of vessels carrying armies of foreigners.

This is one thing that has changed with time, however, and today Corsicans welcome the hordes of visitors who come to enjoy — not to sack — the island's natural splendor. In summer, the airports are busy with jets, the ports with commercial ferries, and new marinas welcome pleasure craft whose sails flap in the summer breezes. All is in place for one to just enjoy the warmth of the Corsican sunshine and beaches, do a little sightseeing or shopping, and watch the sunset while sipping an apéritif at one of the genteel coastal resorts. Or simply tour by car to take in the fantastic vistas. On the other hand, once impenetrable mountain passes have been cleared and now offer spectacular walking routes, bridleways, and cycle paths. The rivers, gorges, and rapids are perfect for kayaking or canoeing. The sharp peaks are a lure to climbers and the mountain air provides a lift for hang-gliders. There are few places better than Corsica to really get out and enjoy the great outdoors.

A BRIEF HISTORY

Ancient Corsica

This island has had a long and complicated human history, which began as early as the seventh millenium B.C. The first settlers were hunter-gatherers and fishermen who traveled to Corsica from the coast of northern Italy. Pottery has been found dating from 7,500 years ago — these pieces are on display in the Musée Départemental at Levie. The archaeological site at Cucuruzzu has been proven to be one of the oldest on the island, dating from 8600 B.C.

Around 3500 B.C., island residents, the *Corsi*, began to harvest crops and domesticate animals. They lived in communities on the valley floors, but traveled with their animals up to high pastures in summer; this cycle was prevalent on Corsica until the last century.

Megaliths dating from this time have been found all across the Mediterranean Sea, and there are some fine examples on Corsica — their dead were buried in stone chambers covered with a mound of earth or *tumulus*, and marked by upright granite stones or *menhir* (from the Breton words for long stone). From the mid-third millennium B.C. coffins were no longer buried but were placed on the ground, marked with a menhir, and covered with a tumulus. These are known as *dolmen*, from the Breton words for long table. Menhirs gradually became more ornate and doubled in size — up to 4 m (13 ft) in height. A third phase from around 2000 B.C. saw faces and bodily details carved into the stones. The examples found around Filitosi represent some of the first large human sculptures in the Western Hemisphere.

Around 1500 B.C. the local architectural style suddenly changed; a series of protective towers were built at sites like

*Explore the prehistoric Dolmen of Fontanaccia —
a reminder of Corsica's tumultuous past.*

Cucurruzu. This became known as the Torréen period
(named for the *torres*, or towers). No one is yet certain
whether the Torréen development came from within the
community or if tower building was brought by a conquer-
ing force from outside Corsica.

Greeks and Romans

In the sixth century B.C. Greeks from the city of Phocaea
arrived to trade and then to settle. They called the island
Kalliste (the beautiful) and made their main base at Alalia
(later changed to Aléria) which became an important trading
post. Wood and metal ores were exported around the Greek
empire, and grapes and olives were grown in the northeastern plains. The beautiful artifacts now found in the museum
at Aléria give evidence of the wealth the Greeks produced

here. The Corsi retreated from this settlement into the more remote regions of the island; this was the beginning of the "twin track" development of Corsica. The east saw more growth and new ideas from outsiders, where the mountainous, less accessible west had fewer outside influences and developed its own steadfast traditions.

Eventually the Greeks came into conflict with the neighboring Etruscans in Italy; a battle in 535 B.C. forced them to leave. The Etruscans vied with the city of Carthage on the African coast for control of Corsica, the Carthaginians eventually being victorious.

The Romans arrived in 259 B.C. They engaged the Carthaginians in the Punic Wars and took Corsica in 230 B.C. The remains of the Roman city of Aléria can still be visited, though the port was eventually suffocated by silt (after

Gaze out at the Mediterranean from the black sand beach beneath the remains of an ancient Genoese tower.

the decline of the Roman Empire). Unlike the Greeks, the Romans enslaved the Corsi people, forcing them to work in Roman farms and mines on the island, or exporting them to other parts of the Roman Empire. It was around this time that the first Corsicans began their fight for self-determination. In the 170s B.C. there was an unsuccessful revolt; almost half of the Corsi population perished. Those who remained headed to the hills to continue to be a thorn in the Roman side.

The Dark Ages

In the fifth century A.D., as the Roman Empire was in its death throes, Aléria suffered a series of malaria epidemics, a devastating fire, and, in 456, Vandal raids from the Danube Valley that finally destroyed the city. Waves of invaders came and went during the Dark Ages, including the Goths and Byzantines. In 774 Corsica came under papal control, though in name only; in reality this offered the island no protection. Forces of Muslim Saracens or Moors arrived in the ninth century and controlled it for 200 years. They were cruel masters who sold the Corsi into slavery, but even so, the Moors' head is still used as a symbol of Corsica to the present day.

After the Moors were vanquished, Rome had little real interest in the island, whereas noblemen from the nearby Italian coast had trading routes to protect from the rampaging Moors. They used Corsica to control the sea passages in the region.

In 1077 they offered Corsica to the Bishop of Pisa, a city in northern Italy. He accepted, but his own power was diminishing and control soon passed to the secular city council. The following years of Pisan rule were on the whole peaceful and beneficial. A number of churches dating

from this time can be found on the island; the loveliest is
Église San Michele de Murato, in the Bevinco Valley southwest of Bastia.

Pisa held the island for 50 years before Genoa began to
wrest it from their clutches. The papal dioceses were trans-
ferred entirely to Genoa; then in 1133 they were split
north/south with Pisa, which only exacerbated the division
within Corsica. Then in 1284 the Genoese soundly beat the
Pisans in battle and took the whole island.

The Genoese Era

Though the Genoese then nominally ruled Corsica for the next

500 years, there were more
than a few problems.
Although they set about fortifying Corsica's main settlements — Bonifacio and Calvi
are stellar examples of their
handiwork — feuds with the
papacy, other ruling dynasties,
and Corsican feudal overlords
saw the balance of power shift
constantly. Throughout the
ensuing centuries the Corsicans went about their lives
at the mercy of the dominant
power of the time. They were
farmers, shepherds, and fishermen caught up in greater

*Pascal Paoli is remembered
and revered as the father
of modern Corsica.*

political and religious conflicts, which their taxes were often used to fund.

The machinations began soon after the Genoese took control. In 1297 the pope gave control of both Corsica and neighboring Sardinia to the King of Aragon (now part of modern Spain) who moved to settle in the major town. Decades of skirmishes with the Genoese followed. In 1358, the peasants began their own domestic revolt, the Sambucuccio Uprising, laying siege to the Aragonese castles. The Genoese forces sided with the patriots and in the aftermath of the victory gave them the captured northeastern Aragonese lands *in commune* with guaranteed grazing rights. The free settlements adopted a form of self-rule. This increased their differences with the southwest, where land and power remained in the hands of feudal lords until 1789. These men controlled by means of family connection and fear; this was the foundation of the tradition of vendetta, in which the family of an injured or dead man can demand revenge down through the generations.

Despite the setback, the Spanish refused to give up their rights on the island and sent a force to regain the lost land. In the early 15th century the Spanish fortified the tiny site at Corte as a new capital, but their efforts finally came to an end in 1434, when their last viceroy was captured and beheaded in Genoa.

However, the Genoese had become overstretched. Involved in a series of disputes on the Italian peninsula, they had no money and little remaining capacity to keep control of the island. In 1453 Corsica was let to the Bank of St. George, to whom the Genoese were in a great deal of debt. The new masters set about fortifying the islands with a series of coastal watchtowers — the remains of over 30 still stand — so the population would have time to head to the hills in the event of attack. Local confidence increased, bringing about a period of economic growth.

In 1553 the French King Henry II took the island. He had allied himself to Hapsburg Emperor Charles V against Genoa; one of his military leaders, Sampiero Corso, a native of Corsica, hoped perhaps to use the situation to the advantage of his homeland. The Genoese were expelled and in 1557 Corsica was assimilated into France. But the treaty that ended the war in 1559 handed the island back to the Genoese. Corso was incensed and organized a popular revolt. After his death in 1567 the Genoese re-established their control.

In 1571, the *Statuti Civili e Criminali di Corsica* were instituted, giving the island both civil and criminal law and an administration ruled by a *consultas*, or public assembly, made up from the ruling noble families. Though civil insurrection happened intermittently, the island saw 150 years of relative stability — until the beginning of the 18th century, when Genoese influence began to wane. Seeing a chance to take control from the ailing power, the Corsicans once again began a war of independence.

An Independent Corsica?

Hostilities began in 1729, and the Genoese cried for help in the face of this growing threat. Emperor Charles VI sent Austrian troops, so the islanders retreated into the mountains to begin a guerrilla war against these foreign forces. In 1732 peace was negotiated, which the Genoese immediately broke. But as Charles had already recalled his troops, the Corsicans seized the opportunity to declare independence in 1735.

There followed a period of power-broking, which the Corsicans would ultimately lose. The Genoese blockaded the island, but rescue came in the form of Baron Théodore von Neuhoff of Westphalia. He arrived with a ship full of food and weapons for the freedom fighters, who really had no choice but to accept the supplies and the accompanying condition that the Baron be conferred the title "King of Corsica." However, when the Italians asked the French to help them quell the rebellion, Théodore took this as sign that he had bitten off more than he could chew and retreated to the mainland. The French initially tried to negotiate with the islanders but talks collapsed

The tri-color French flag flies above the traditional Moor's-head flag of Corsica.

and they went to battle, defeating the Corsican army. The French were then recalled, but as soon as they departed fighting broke out again between the Corsicans and Genoese. Patriot Giampietro Gaffori stormed the Genoese citadel at Corte, and in 1746 was proclaimed leader of a new Corsican Republic — even though the Genoese still occupied a number of coastal fortresses. When Gaffori was murdered in 1753, Pascal Paoli was elected leader and began to build a strong, independent nation.

Paoli is beloved to this day by his countrymen — not only because he was a brave leader, but because he had the best interest of all Corsicans at heart. He outlawed the vendetta and organized a democratic legislative process, a codified legal process that diminished the power of the noble families, and an education system, including the foundation of a University at Corte in 1765.

French Corsica

Finally in 1768 the Genoese realized that they no longer had the resources to rule Corsica. However, instead of recognizing the independence of the island under Paoli, they sought to recoup some last return from their fiefdom and ceded the island to the French under the Treaty of Versailles. A French fleet set sail to subdue the astonished and angry populace, who were ready once again to take up arms to fight for their island. The battle of Ponte Nouvo on 9 May 1769 was the decisive moment, when massive French forces finally defeated the Corsican army. The very same year, Napoléon Bonaparte was born in the newly French city of Ajaccio.

When the French Revolution shook Europe in 1789, Paoli made one final attempt to free his homeland by calling on the English for aid. In 1794 the Anglo Corsican Constitution came into being. However, the English bowed to French pressure and in 1796 Corsica returned to France. Paoli went into exile, to die in London in 1807. By 1811 Corsica was united as one *department* of France, with Ajaccio as its capital, but to the present day, underground independence fighters have worked for freedom from outside control.

Corsica became a rural backwater of the democratic French Republic. Though attempts were made to develop the island, they were met with disinterest, or even distrust, by the local people. French was introduced as the official language; the Corsi language, a fusion of Latin and Italian, was suppressed.

The university at Corte — regarded as a hotbed of subversion — was closed. Throughout the 19th and early 20th centuries, young people migrated in great numbers for better opportunities abroad.

The Late 20th Century

Since World War II, Corsica has been fighting against what local people regard as internal colonialism. The institution of Algerian self-determination in 1962 in particular struck a chord with the Corsicans. At the same time France began a process of economic and political de-centralization and regionalization, and Corsica demanded privileges and subsidies to repair wartime damage and kick-start their economy.

The bell tower of this Romanesque church dates back to the 12th century.

Pressure groups also began to develop. In 1963 a Corsican student organization was created in order to to stop the depopulation of their island and to promote the teaching of Corsican language and history in schools. In 1964 doctors Edmond and Max Simeoni founded the Comité d'Etudes et de Défense des Intérêts de la Corse, whose aim was to protect Corsican interests within greater France. Soon there were numerous factions, each with a different aim. At the forefront of these was Azzione per la Rinascita (ARC), who campaigned for infrastructure development. It also lobbied for the reopening of Corsica University at Corte.

In 1970 Corsica became the 22nd region of France, and in 1975 was divided into two administrative departments, la Corse-du-Sud in the south and Haute-Corse in the north. But development was not moving along according to plan and, as progress was painfully slow, the patience of the ARC began to wear thin.

In the late 1970s a series of environmental scandals rocked Corsica. It was discovered that an Italian company had been dumping toxic waste in the straights between the Italian mainland and Corsica. The French government appeared indifferent to the problem and in fact had plans to dump its own waste off the coast. In 1975 the main import agent for Corsican wine in France was declared bankrupt and a number of major producers were ruined. As evidence of fraud mounted, a number of ARC members occupied the offices of the bankrupt companies in Aléria, and the French government reacted by sending in riot troops. In the resulting battle two policemen were killed. Following this a number of more extreme nationalist groups began a campaign of violence.

Other parties tried to work within the system to raise the profile of the island, and have made changes in the late 20th century. In 1981 the University of Corsica was reopened. In 1982 and 1991 political and administrative changes created the Statut Particulier de la Corse and the Collectivité Territoriale de Corse (CTC), giving Corsica a unique place within the French constitution laws. This, however, was not independence.

In February 1998 Corsica's governor Préfet Claude Érignac was shot and killed as he made his way to a concert in Ajaccio. He had been leading an enquiry into the misappropriation of millions of francs, given as subsidies to the island. An official enquiry later that year concluded that several leading Corsican figures, with the complicity of the Regional Assembly and the French government, had defrauded the taxpayers. Those involved were promptly arrested. The elections for the Corsican regional assembly held in March were declared void in December 1998. Though all independence groups distanced themselves from the assassination, it was followed by an increase in civil disruption.

In May 1999, the French Prime Minister Lionel Jospin visited the island to address the Corsican Assembly. He delivered a blunt message; Corsica could not expect autonomy, and there would be no progress on the economic front unless it renounced violence. His visit was marked by an island-wide strike and bomb attacks on government buildings. There were more attacks in the fall of 1999, all on government buildings, and all in the dead of night, which ensured no injuries. It seemed that there was little will to compromise on either side. But just before Christmas 1999, there was a meeting between Mr. Jospin and the major Corsican politicians. A few days later, the main separatist groups announced an open-ended cease-fire, signaling a willingness to negotiate.

These political differences have little effect on the day-to-day activities on Corsica; most visitors see little evidence of Corsican nationalism other than painted slogans on rocks and road signs. These are an indication that, although its complex past cannot be forgotten, Corsica lives entirely for the present.

WHERE TO GO

Corsica is an island of immense variety. Miles of beautiful sandy beach in the east balance the rocky coves of the west. The urbane and chic town streets contrast with the empty splendor of the mountains. Plains of vine and fruit orchards lie side-by-side with the acres of pine and chestnut forest, and hillsides of fragrant wild *maccia* bound meadowlands. Each of these areas also changes with the seasons. In the winter the island sleeps save for skiers and snowboarders. Spring sees the hillsides awash with wildflowers, migrating birds stopping off on their way north, and piglets, calves, and kids being born. Summer's heat slows the pace, and thousands of tourists flock to the marinas and beaches while the sunshine ripens the rich crops. Fall brings the harvest of vines, olives, and chestnuts, and the colors of ochre and gold. All these attributes make Corsica a fascinating place to explore.

This guide divides Corsica into four sections; the southwest is covered first, with the primary administrative town of Corsica, Ajaccio, as the focus. Second is the southeast, which includes the town of Bonifacio. The northeast and Bastia follow, and then the northwest and its main town, Calvi. Excursions along the coast and into the interior will further cover the natural wonders to be found on Corsica.

THE SOUTHWEST

The southwestern area of Corsica is marked by its most French town, birthplace of the Republic's hero, Napoléon Bonaparte. In the Neolithic era, this area hosted thriving communities of hunter-gatherers who have left numerous signs of their existence and lifestyle. Later, it was the heartland of the Corsican vendetta or blood feud, at its most prevalent at the town of Sartène farther south. Feudal control reigned here, the land controlled by only a few powerful families, until the late 18th century.

Ajaccio

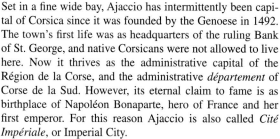

Set in a fine wide bay, Ajaccio has intermittently been capital of Corsica since it was founded by the Genoese in 1492. The town's first life was as headquarters of the ruling Bank of St. George, and native Corsicans were not allowed to live here. Now it thrives as the administrative capital of the Région de la Corse, and the administrative *département* of Corse de la Sud. However, its eternal claim to fame is as birthplace of Napoléon Bonaparte, hero of France and her first emperor. For this reason Ajaccio is also called *Cité Impériale*, or Imperial City.

Those arriving by ship or plane get a breathtaking view of the whole town. Its pastel-colored buildings spread along the coastline and up into the verdant hills behind. Many of the taller buildings are modern apartment blocks, but hundreds of potted plants and colorful awnings soften the rather square lines and so don't ruin the view. Although it is a large settlement by Corsican standards, Ajaccio has the feel of a small and friendly provincial town. Pretty avenues, town squares,

The Macchia

Corsica is covered with a blanket of wild plants, a low scrub called *macchia* (or *maquis* in French), never more than 3 m (10 ft) high. The exact combination differs according to soil composition and altitude; however, each mixture imparts an exotic scent of wild herbs (marjoram, fennel, basil, and thyme) and of flowers (myrtle, mastic, or broom). It is said that a Corsican would know he was in his homeland even with his eyes closed because the smell is so distinctive.

streetside cafés, and numerous pretty boutiques make it a pleasure to stroll around.

The harbor is protected by a long wall, or *mole*, called **Jetée de la Citadelle**, behind which is the modern ferry port, the major hub of activity in Ajaccio. Several ships arrive daily from France and Italy. Just next door, Port Plaisance Tino Rossi caters to sailboats and pleasure craft of all kinds, including visiting vessels from around the Mediterranean Sea and beyond. The shallowest and most sheltered part of the harbor, Port Abri, is reserved for local fishing boats, which will

Pleasure craft and sailboats moor in the Port de Plaisance, a charming little marina.

head farther out to sea when conditions are good. Although catches are diminishing, the daily fishmarket stalls on the quayside will amaze with the variety of local seafood available. Along the quayside are several restaurants that take advantage of the bounty from the sea around them. Any one of these is a great place to have lunch or dinner and watch the world go by.

The land end of the mole attaches to **The Citadel**, a small fortress built by the French when Sampiero Corso captured Ajaccio in 1553. When the Genoese reclaimed the town they further fortified the point; its strong walls are still in excellent repair, for it is used even now as the local administrative headquarters for the French army. Around and beyond the citadel is a small town beach and promenade. Look out for the tiny **Musée Capitellu** on your right. This interesting museum tells the story of Ajaccio though the experiences of a fictitious town family; you'll see artifacts typical of households in the city through the ages. Beyond the museum, at the start of the promenade on the right, you'll find the modern Neo-Classical façade of Ajaccio Casino.

Away from the water's edge, stroll down some of the interesting streets of the old town to look at the tall houses with their painted shutters. The family home of the Bonapartes and birthplace of Napoléon, **Maison Bonaparte**, stands on a narrow street which has since been named rue Maison Bonaparte. Surrounded by other homes in the present day, it had fewer neighbors during Napoléon's childhood; etchings of the house at that time can be found on the top floor. The large Bonaparte family — Napoléon was one

A few local sunbathers take in some rays on a small beach beneath the ramparts and watch tower of the Citadel.

of 11 children — lived on the middle floor with a family of close relatives above. Unfortunately, the house was badly damaged when Charles Bonaparte (Napoléon's father) took the side of the French against Paoli in 1793; Marie-Letitzia Bonaparte had the house totally refurbished on their return in 1797, so much of the decoration dates from after Napoléon's time here. The Emperor returned to his boyhood home for the last time in 1799, on his way back from a campaign in Egypt. The rooms display furniture and wall and ceiling decorations typical of the period. One piece of original wallpaper remains on display. More fascinating, perhaps, is the family tree of the Bonapartes, displayed on the top floor along with two death masks of the Emperor taken at St. Helena.

> Corsicans offer one kiss on each cheek in greeting.

The nearby **Cathédrale de Notre-Dame** was built in 1582 in Romanesque style. Its simple construction and small size belie Ajaccio's current importance as administrative center of the island. Napoléon was baptized here and hoped to be entombed here after his death, but his contribution to France was too great for the French people to agree to his last wish. The church contains a marble maitre-autel given to the church by Napoléon's sister, Elisa Bacciocchi, and *Vierge au Sacré-Coeur*, a painting by Delacroix. Down the street is the tiny Église St-Érasme, or Church of Saint Erasmus, patron saint of sailors.

Just a short walk from Maison Bonaparte, **Place Maréchal Foch** is the center of the old town. A pleasant square, it is lined with palm trees, and benches set under the cooling branches are a favorite place for older Ajaccians to meet and chat. At the western end of the square is a fountain topped with a statue of Napoléon dressed as the Roman emperor, complete with draped toga; it is named for the lions that lie at his feet. Several curved boulevards lead off from here, making for a typically Mediterranean French vista.

At the opposite end of the square is the **Hôtel de Ville** (Town Hall), painted a pretty pastel pink, a lovely contrast to the square's green palm fronds. On the second floor you will find the **Musée Napoléonien**, which displays numerous mementos of the man himself and of other luminaries in the Bonaparte family.

Behind the town hall and immediately across from the ferry terminal, **Place César Campinchi** hosts a large market every morning. This is a great place to buy delicious Corsican foods such as pre-

Napoléon is Corsica's most famous son — here he presides over Place Foch.

served meats, cheeses, jam, honey, wine, and a range of fruit and vegetables: perfect for a picnic lunch. You can sample many items before you buy, and the stallholders are only too happy to go into detail about the produce — in French of course. Across the street from the market, the local tourist office is located on Rue du Roi-Jérôme on the landward side of the square.

One block west of the marketplace, Rue Cardinal Fesch, a shopping thoroughfare, is named after a maternal uncle of Napoléon's who, apart from his important position in the Catholic Church, was also a lover of art. His astonishing collection is housed in the old cardinal's palace at number 52, where a statue of the cardinal graces the entrance square of **Musée Fesch**. The galleries are filled with many major pieces. The second floor displays Italian art from the 14th to the 16th centuries, the third floor European art of the 17th and 18th centuries. This collection is second only in France to the Louvre in Paris for Italian art, and the Venetian and Florentine schools are well represented, with works by Giovanni Bellini (1430–1516) and Sandro Botticelli (1440–1510). Examples of other artists work represented here include *l'Homme au Gant* by Titian (1488–1576) and *Midas à la Source du Pactole* by Nicholas Poussin (1594–1665). The lower ground floor has a collection of Napoléon memorabilia, including souvenir statues created in his likeness, along with personal artifacts of Cardinal Fesch. The gallery also keeps a research library of 50,000 volumes, col-

The Musée Fesch galleries house many famous works from different periods of European art history.

lected by Lucien Bonaparte when he was Minister of the Interior in 1801.

The **Bonaparte family chapel** sits beside Musée Fesch. Built in 1857 by Napoléon III, many family members lie here — though not the most famous Bonaparte, who rests in Paris at Les Invalides.

Heading west from Place Maréchal Foch, a short street leads to **Place Diamant**, officially Place Géneral du Gaulle, and the beginning of the modern town of Ajaccio. The place is a wide, open space often used by skateboarders, or young children on bicycles. A statue of Napoléon astride a horse graces the seaward flank. Several wide boulevards intersect here, including **Cours Napoléon**, where you will find the post office (*la Poste*) along with several fine boutiques. Follow Cours Grandval up a small hill to **Place Austerlitz**, where you will find another statue of Napoléon, this time dressed in full military uniform.

Excursions Inland

In the hills 5 km (3 miles) above town is **Les Milelli**, country home of the Bonaparte family. Still a lovely setting today, this was a peaceful retreat for the family during the heat of the Corsican summers — and a necessary hideaway they sheltered in while being pursued by Paoli's men.

Ajaccio itself has no proper beach, but several sandy bays can be found just a short distance to the west. Some of the finer hotels are situated along the coast road here — the route is serviced by the *petit train* (a small motorized vehicle with carriages in the shape of a miniature train) during peak season. The train stops at Point de Parata, where the **Iles Sanguinaires** reach out into the Golfe d'Ajaccio. There is a café here, and a footpath that offers a pleasant stroll to the farthest point out on the bay, Point de Sanguinaires.

South from Ajaccio, the main road leads past Campo dell'Oro Airport and a sandy beach, on its seaward side, where there are numerous watersports available. At 21 km (12 miles) along route 193 toward Bastia there is a tortoise sanctuary called **A Cupulatta**. Situated on $2^1/_2$-hectares ($6^1/_2$-acres), there are over 2000 of the creatures on view; the park also operates a breeding program for rare species. The sanctuary is open to the public from April to November.

Beyond the airport, there is a traffic circle with signs indicating the route to **Porticcio** on the D55 road. The

Beach-goers can find refreshment at the quaint cafés of Route Les Sanguinaires.

first site of interest on this road is the **Aqua Cyrné Gliss**, a water park with slides and plunge pools — great fun for the child in everyone. It leads next to the south side of the Golfe d'Ajaccio, where there is a long sandy bay, the **Plage de Porticcio**, well serviced with cafés, restaurants, and beach shops. If playing in the water isn't on the agenda for the day, carry on to the **Punta di Sette Nave**, where you can explore the rocky coves below the Genoese Tour de l'Isolella. There are good views across the bay to Ajaccio from here as well.

The N196 leads east into the hills; 12 km (8 miles) down the road is the village of Cauro and the junction to D27, which heads to the village of **Bastelica**. This is the birthplace of freedom fighter Sampiero Corso, who led French forces against the Genoese in 1553. The village has a bronze statue of their famous son, and his birthplace is open to visitors. The 33-km (20-mile) drive to this village, up into the hills, is a pleasant journey through pretty countryside; on your return to Ajaccio try another scenic route, via the D3 down through the **Gorge de Prunelli**. There are majestic views across the Lac du Tolla (Lake Tolla) to the mountains in the east. The whole trip takes around three hours and is a worthwhile excursion.

Continuing on the N196 south from Cauro will take you through the hills surrounding the Taravo River and into the area of Corsica that has been inhabited since prehistoric times. Corsica is now regarded as the most important area in Europe for megalithic statue art; there are several sites to visit between here and the south coast. Although not large,

Mérimée and Corsican Folklore

In his role as Inspector General for Public Buildings, Prosper Mérimée was given the task of cataloguing the main architectural treasures of every province in France. He came to Corsica in 1839 to begin a comprehensive inventory of historic and ancient sites. He visited sites such as Filitosa and Aléria before writing a report of his findings under the title *Les Notes d'un voyage en Corse*.

Mérimée also fell in love with Corsican folklore during his time here. He wrote a novel, *Colomba*, telling of a family caught up in a Corsican blood feud in the Sartenais region, which became a best seller in France when it was published in 1840. This vivid picture painted in words illuminated the rituals and rules of life on Corsica, and made the island "the land of the vendetta."

the sites are fascinating in that they seem more like prehistoric remains in Brittany, thousands of kilometers to the north, than other, closer Mediterranean remains. Many sites are on private land with footpath access and most of the signs are old and difficult to read. There is no charge to view most of the sites, and there is no one to manage them on a day-to-day basis; respect the surrounding area and close farm gates after you have passed through them.

Look for the turnoff for **Filitosa**, the most important site on Corsica, as you drive over the summit and drop toward the Golfe de Valinco; there is a sign for Sollarco and Filitosa on the right. This site is managed by the Cesari family, who own the surrounding land. In the 1950s they invited Roger Grosjean, an archaeologist, to study the area; it was from his research that modern theories of ancient Corsican history have been formulated.

The unusual prehistoric stone formations found on Corsica have puzzled visitors and researchers for years.

The Filitosa site sits atop a small hill and stretches some 400 m (1,312 ft) into the surrounding countryside. Evidence of human habitation here dates from 6000 B.C., though the main attractions are several menhirs (standing stones), some decorated with faces, which date from 3300 B.C. to 1800 B.C. It is thought these statues represented real people, and acted as memorials to them after death. During the Bronze Age, 1800–700 B.C., the site was fortified with a toréen and the population lived in stone huts, the remains of which can still be seen. The Cesari family have created an impressive museum with finds from all eras of the site's history, including Bronze Age tools and later Greek and Roman pottery. An English-language pamphlet about the site is available for purchase.

South of Filitosa is the Golf de Valinco. From N196 there are impressive views as one drops through the village of **Olmeto**, set high on the hillside. Impressive old family homes sit beside the now busy road; when they were erected, traffic would have been just carts and buggies pulled by donkeys or horses. Eventually the road swings around the head of the bay at sea level to the port of **Propriano**. There are several beautiful sandy beaches at either side of the town and a number of seafood restaurants on the small marina, which makes this a good spot to stop for lunch.

Beyond Propriano the road begins to climb again into the Ortolo hills of the Sartenais region, considered even by Corsicans to be the heartland of the island. The families here have strong roots; it was here that the vendetta, or blood feud, for which Corsica is famed originally developed. Having no recourse through the law — which favored the Genoese nobility — the Corsicans began to take it into their own hands. Death was the ultimate punishment, and the knife or the bullet settled many a score. A family wronged was to be avenged, and it is said that these feuds have been carried to the present day — though hostilities officially ceased in 1834. As visitors you won't even be aware of the political machinations, and the Sartenais region is just as friendly as any other part of Corsica. The bullet holes in the road signs are more the result of frustrated hunters than of any jealous husbands.

Take a short detour (4 km/2½ miles) at the D268 to find the Genoese bridge of **Spin'a Cavallu** spanning the Rizzanese River. The bridge, originally erected in the 13th century and of beautiful yet simple design, is probably the best preserved on the island, as it was renovated in 1993. It is easy to imagine donkeys laden with goods climbing the steep rise; carts or other wheeled vehicles would not fit across the span. The river water is clean and clear here, with pools for swimming. Picnic tables allow you to make the most of the view, so stay a while and enjoy the quiet.

As the road climbs farther up into the hills you will get your first glimpse of **Sartène** (Sarte), described by Mérime as "the most Corsican of the Corsican towns." Its dour buildings cling to the hillside, and, as you enter the town, you come up close to the rocks on which the ancient settlement was built. Though historically an important trading post and rest stop on the route south, the town could be an impregnable fortress if

This Genoese bridge reflects some of the unique architecture in the region.

Little villages dot the hillsides of Corsica, providing countless picture-postcard Mediterranean vistas.

need be. Throughout the Middle Ages it was the center of a powerful fiefdom, which held itself apart from the rest of the island. Later the town itself divided into two warring factions, those who lived within the ancient walls and those beyond.

The oldest part of town, **Santa Anna**, is a tiny warren of narrow alleys bounded by five- and six-story buildings with small doors and tiny windows set inside high thick walls. It is possible to imagine yourself back in the 16th century as you walk deeper into this maze of gray granite. There are many dead ends, which were designed to confuse raiders or pirates — now they simply confuse visitors — and several tiny squares where in times past, residents would have gathered. Today children still play here; many of the small apartments are occupied by families in the present day.

Enter through an arched stone gateway that you'll find between the cafés and war memorial of **Place de la Libération**.

The church of Sainte-Marie, on the right, is the central focus of the **Catenacciu procession**. Held every year on Good Friday, a barefoot, red-cloaked penitent must walk through the streets carrying a 32 kg (70 lb) wooden cross and wearing a 14 kg (30 lb) chain around his neck (*catenacciu* means "the chained one"), emulating the suffering of Christ on his journey to Golgotha. The procession takes place at 9:30pm; the streets are lit with thousands of candles in windows or carried by hand. The priest, following the penitent, recites the Stations of the Cross and the faithful follow behind in silent prayer.

The **Hôtel de Ville** (once the palace of the Genoese Governor) spans the huge entrance gate of the town. Beyond the gate a turn to the left leads to a small *échauguette*, a lookout post, with views across the narrow valley into the countryside beyond.

The area called **Borgo** lying outside the walls is home to several huge family mansions. Walk the surrounding streets and stairways to catch a glimpse of their detail. These families, known as the "sgio," once exerted an influence, through

The faded faces of the Alignments de Stantari remain on ancient stone megaliths in the Sartenais countryside.

their bloodline, difficult to understand in the 21st century. Their rivalry with families of Santa Anna was at the heart of many vendettas, and reached into every village in the region — to cousins, employees, and friends. Each family had a clan, and each clan had a rival clan. And so it went, until the bloodletting was stopped by official decree in 1834.

Take the narrow steps to the **Musée de Préhistoire Corse** (Corsican Pre-historical Museum) found just off Boulevard J. Nicholai in the old town prison, which dates from 1843. The collection spans almost 9,000 years of Corsican history, from 7000 B.C. to the 16th century, and has several important pieces from the Neolithic age, including sculptures and jewelry gathered from surrounding sites in the Sartenais. Photographs record all the major sites on the island — useful if you want to know what to look for as you explore — and there is a detailed, chronological explanation of the history of the island, although the explanations are all in French.

The Sartenais countryside does not offer the drama of the high mountain scenery, but it is pretty farmland with grazing cattle and small fields of vines. Scattered across the rolling hills are several Neolithic sites; take the D48 road just south of town, off the main Bonifacio road, to find several which you can tour with ease. Three separate sites along a circular route have together come to be known as **Mégalithes de Cauria**. A visit to all three takes around an hour to complete. Take a left 10 km (6 miles) along D48 to a dusty parking lot, then follow the signs to the Dolmen de Fontanaccia, the best preserved funerary chamber on Corsica. Five minutes away, are the Alignments of Stantari, a series of Megalithic statues with the faint impressions of faces and weapons. Take the footpath behind this site to explore the Alignments of Renaggiu, just a ten-minute stroll across the fields. This group of standing stones is set in a small copse.

The most remarkable collection of standing stones, the **Alignements de Palaggiu**, are a little way farther south on the D48. They can be found along a farm path off to the right, though there is no signpost and they are not visible from the road, making them difficult to locate. Stop at the Domaine Moscani winery — practically the only building in the neighborhood — to ask directions. There are over 250 stones at this site, lying around as if thrown by a giant's hand. Only a few have visible features (many may have been weathered smooth) but the sheer scale of the site is impressive enough.

The D48 ends at the tiny settlement of Tizzano on the coast, but access to the impressive castle is difficult, as the road is unpaved. It is possible to walk along the coastline here if you leave the car at the end of the tarmac.

The main road from Sartène (N196) leads on inexorably toward Bonifacio. Just before the road hits the coast, turn right at the Bocca di Curali (with a restaurant at the roadside) and head down to the sandy bay of **Roccapina**. The hills bounding the bay are worth exploring. On the left is a Genoese tower and a curious rock formation, the **Rocher du Lion**, so named because of its shape. On the right hillside are megalithic remains. The surrounding countryside is a natural reserve with many bird habitats; spring is the best time to spot these creatures.

THE SOUTHEAST

Chalk cliffs characterize the landscape of the far south, with beautiful beaches along the east coast. Two Genoese citadels mark the major settlements, with one, Bonifacio, located at a spectacular site. Inland, high mountain passes, pretty villages, and beautiful, unspoiled pine forests are all waiting to be explored.

Bonifacio

Bonifacio is the jewel in Corsica's crown. It is not the only medieval citadel on the island, but its setting atop a chalk outcrop over 60 m (197 ft) high makes it one of the most unusual and dramatic in Europe. Bounded by water on three sides, the rock has been strategically important for many centuries — it was initially settled by the Greeks and the Romans. In 828 the city was given its name by Boniface, the Marquis of Tuscany. Throughout its history, Bonifacio has been fought over by the Pisans, Genoese, and Aragonese, as well as pirates who traveled the Mediterranean in search of slaves and booty. Finds from pre-history include a skeleton from 6750 B.C., named Le Dame de Bonifacio by locals, on view at a museum in the town of Levie farther north (see

Bonifacio is home to another Genoese citadel, used gallantly to keep out all sorts of unwanted visitors.

*Corsican dining, influenced by both French and Italian,
utilizes the bounty of fresh goods available on the island.*

page 48). The present fortifications at Bonifacio date from
1195. Built by the Genoese, they kept everyone, including
the Corsicans, out. To this day the citadel defies the power of
the sea, which pounds the rocks below. Surely it will eventually lose the battle, but for now it looms majestically from
its perch, and the views from its ramparts are magnificent.

The rock on which the citadel is perched shelters a natural harbor — actually an inlet — called the **Goulet de
Bonifacio**, which is 1,500 m (1 mile) long. Very popular
with yachtsmen and pleasure boaters, it is thought that this
was Lamos harbor, which sheltered Odysseus and his fleet
from a storm, in Homer's *Odyssey*. Unfortunately, the local
Laestrygon people were cannibals and Odysseus had to
make a hasty retreat back out to sea, but you are bound to get

a warmer welcome from the Bonifacians. A fleet of small boats wait to take you out to view the cliffs and caves of the coastline, as well as the citadel, and the harborfront is lined with restaurants and a few hotels — perfect as a base from which to visit the citadel above.

You can reach the citadel by car (parking is available outside the walls), or walk from the harbor up the steps of **Montée Rastello**; they are wide and not steep, but there are quite a few of them. Alternatively, take the petit train from the head of the quay, which will get you to the citadel in a few minutes. (This is a popular option, so be prepared to wait in line.) Those who take the train do miss one of the highlights of the citadel — entering through the huge **Porte De Gênes**, built in the 16th century. The pulley system for the drawbridge, which could close off the city from raiders, is still in place, but the huge doors now stay permanently open. There are beautiful **views from Col Saint Roch**, a small headland to the east, of the clear blue-green water and the people sunbathing on the rocks below — steps lead down to the water's edge. From here there are also clear views to Sardinia, the Italian island just 12 km (7$\frac{1}{2}$ miles) to the south.

Once through the Porte de Gênes, a maze of narrow streets begs exploration, offering history, great restaurants, and interesting boutiques and souvenir stores. At the **Place d'Armes**, the tops of several huge grain silos, used for storage in medieval times, are visible. To your right and left are the Bastions de l'Etandard, with views down to the harbor. These were the main defense of the Porte de Gênes in times past and now house an exposition about the citadel's history within their ramparts.

Many of the four- and five-story houses that line the tangled streets date from the 14th and 15th centuries; their narrow, vertiginous stone stairways are worn with the footfalls of numerous occupants from eras past. These steps and the homes' small windows were designed as a further line of defense should the citadel be overrun.

Toward the top of **Rue Longue**, near the silo heads, plaques mark two houses where emperors once stayed. On the right is number 4, where Napoléon slept between January and March of 1793 when he was a Lieutenant-Colonel in the Corsican army. In 1541 Charles V spent several nights at number 7 when his ship was driven ashore in a storm. To the left of Rue Longue is **Rue du Corps du Garde**, where you can see the rear of the **Église Sainte Marie Majeure** and the distinctive arcades which link it to surrounding buildings. These arcades collected rainwater, which was stored underneath the loggia at the front of the church. The cistern has now been transformed into a conference room.

The church itself, constructed in the late 13th century, is interesting, its design illustrating a transition between Romanesque and Gothic styles. Inside, its beautifully painted ceilings show signs of age. The loggia, at which important declarations were read to the population and town councilors handed down judgements, was renovated between 1983 and 1987 using traditional methods.

Facing the church is the **Pallazzu Publicu**, housing the Musée d'Art et d'Histoire. The museum displays numerous objects of value including 17th-century Italian tiles, rosaries, and a third-century sarcophagus, but, unfortunately, it is only open from July until the end of August each year.

To the left of Rue du Corps du Garde is **Rue Doria**, filled with cafés and souvenir stores. Walk past the tiny chapel of **St. John the Baptist** and then turn onto **Rue St. Dominique**. On the right are several houses with ornate shields above the doors, indicating that the houses belonged to the Salineri family. Beyond on the left is the plain façade of the **Maison de la Miséricorde**, a hospice founded in the 13th century. At the end of Rue St. Dominique is a small marketplace with a **bronze statue** commemorating the fallen of the French Foreign Legion. Following the independence of Algeria in 1963, the foreign legion made their headquarters at Bonifacio, occupying much of the headland beyond the marketplace. Since their departure, many of the buildings in this area — a part of Bonifacio called **Le Bosco** — lie in decay, though some are still used by the French military. Footpaths through this area lead to the very western end of the outcrop for majestic views and magnificent sunsets.

Bonifacio, a quaint town perched precariously upon the chalk cliffs.

Look out for a small chapel just before the entrance to the military area. This is the **Church of St. Dominique**, begun by the Knights Templar in 1270 and completed by the Dominican order. The interior of the church is decorated with paintings of the Fifteen Mysteries of the Rosary, and the huge wooden sculpture depicting the flaying of St. Barthélemy is carried through the streets in the Bonifacio Good Friday procession.

Although the ordinary people of Bonifacio could only enter or leave the citadel via the Porte de Gênes, there was actually one other entrance. A narrow flight of steps was cut into the chalk cliff on the south side of the citadel to allow members of the ruling family to come and go in secret. You can now walk the same path, down the **Escalier du Roi d'Aragon** (Steps of the King of Aragon), to a small jetty and footpath. Views of the steps are also impressive from the water on a **tour boat**, where you can see the flight rising from sea level to the town above.

Several companies offer trips from the harbor out to the cliffs (*falaises*) and caves along the coast. In summer you can also take trips to the **Iles Lavezzi**, just off the southeast coast and only one hour away by boat. The islands are uninhabited and the rocky beaches offer endless terrain to explore.

Outlying Attractions

Though Bonifacio has no beach, there are several excellent options within an hour's travel north along the eastern coast. They are all extremely popular in high season, when the sand disappears beneath thousands of beach towels and lounge chairs. The nearest is at the **Gulf of Sant' Amanza**. South of here (east of Bonifacio, and an enjoyable walk along the cliffs from the citadel) are the ruins of a Roman villa at **Piantarella**.

The beaches of the southeastern corner are probably the best on the island, with fine golden sand backed by vegetation that offers shade in the heat of the day, and clear water of azure blue and jade green reminiscent of a Caribbean destination. The **Golfe de Santa Giulia**, just off the N198, has an *étang* (salt lake) where seabirds gather, and several fine hotels if you wish to stay a while. **Palombaggia**, a little way northeast, comprises several bays of beautiful sand interspersed with outcrops of huge sandstone rocks worn smooth by wind and water. Sand dunes behind the beach, now a nature reserve, have footpaths for exploring the low scrub vegetation that birds and lizards make their home. In the ochre hills beyond the dunes are hotels, private villas, and a small selection of restaurants.

Following the coast road past Palombaggia will eventually bring you to the southern side of the Golfe de Porto-Vecchio, with pretty views across the bay to the town of Porto-Vecchio itself. To reach town, rejoin the N198; you'll pass a wetland area in the shallows of the gulf. In the summer months, salt is mined on the flats — this is an ancient industry now being revived because of the high quality of the salt produced here.

Rent a kayak and take a solitary tour around the rock formations in the bay at Palombaggia.

Working fishing boats adorn the harbor — the Corsicans have always enjoyed the many fruits of the sea.

Porto-Vecchio was fortified during the 16th century, but apart from a wall on the seaward side, little remains today — it was badly damaged in a battle between the Spanish (Aragonese) and Genoese in 1564. The settlement, surrounded by wetlands, suffered bouts of malaria until the 20th century, when the mosquitoes carrying the disease were eradicated. The attraction of the town in modern times is its large marina, and the streets throng with Italian and French visitors in August. The area offers several boutiques selling up-market fashions, and it is a pleasure to stroll the network of streets to browse before eating at any one of the many good restaurants.

The N198 road next passes **Torre**, the site said to have given the name *torréen* to the fortified Neolithic structures all across Corsica. Past Torre the road eventually leads to Bastia, but our journey leads inland, into the Alta Rocca, or High Rocca, region within the Parc Naturel Régional de la Corse.

The Rocca family were very powerful in south Corsica during medieval times; they controlled much of the territory from a base at Sartène (see page 36). The region itself has a recorded history far longer than that of the family that gave it its name, and offers some beautiful natural attractions to explore. It is well served by GR footpaths for long and short walks. To reach Alta Rocca, travel north from Bonifacio via Figari, or northwest from Porto Vecchio, though there is also a route east from Sartène.

The capital of the Alta Rocca region is the small town of **Levie**. The highlight of this tiny community is the **Musée Départemental**, just behind the Town Hall (Hôtel de Ville). Finds from all across the region and all eras of history are displayed in three rooms here, includng the **Dame de Bonifacio**, a female human skeleton dating from 6750 B.C., which is the oldest yet discovered on Corsica. She is display-ed under glass exactly as she was laid in death. The locals are equally proud of an ivory statue of Christ sculpted by the school of Niccola de Betto Bardi, known as Donatello: It was presented to Levie by a native of the town, Felice Peretti, who joined the church and in 1585 became Pope Sixtus V.

This sleepy little village is the resting place of the **Dame de Bonifacio.**

A little farther south, the village of **Carbini** is said to have the oldest *campanile* (bell tower) on Corsica. Set apart from the baptistery, it was built in the early part of the 12th century.

North of Levie are two important pre-historic sites. Both **Cucuruzzu** and **Capula** were inhabited until relatively modern times (the middle ages and the 17th century, respectively), and can both be visited at one time; the walk will take about 1¹/₂ hours, including time to explore the attractions. The entrance fee includes a headset and audiotape with commentary on the life of the people who once inhabited these sites.

Though there is evidence of settlement as early as 6800 B.C., the main fortifications at Cucuruzzu date from 1800 B.C. The circular walls are 5 m (16 ft) high and 3 m (10 ft) thick, with chambers for living and for storing food. The people here lived as hunter-gatherers until 5,000 years ago, when they began to cultivate crops and raise animals. Capula was fortified at a later date, but the history of the two ran parallel for many generations. Both settlements were left untouched as Corsica was swept by Greek, Roman, and barbarian settlers, and this pure development makes them a useful source of information for archaeologists. Capula was a powerful fortification until the ninth century A.D. when it lost a power struggle with the Roccas and became a part of their growing fiefdom.

Traveling northeast from Levie leads higher into the mountains. You will share the road with cyclists undertaking one of the most challenging ascents on Corsica: the trip up to the **Col de Bavella**. The *col*, or pass, at 1,218 m (3,996 ft), is the starting point for many mountain hikes and climbs (it is on the GR20 hiking route) and offers panoramic views of the surrounding countryside. At the peak of the col stands the statue of **Notre Dame des Neiges** (Our Lady of the

All-terrain biking has become a popular mode of navigating the mountainous countryside.

Snows), placed here to protect climbers and hikers; she is surrounded by candles and messages placed here in prayers of hope and of thanks.

High above the col are the **Aiguilles de Bavella**, a range of jagged mountain peaks named "needles" in French. The sheer granite rocks, bare on their southern façade, are a magnificent sight. One of the most photographed sights on Corsica, they look prettiest with the village of **Zonza** in the foreground. The stopping point for many organized tours through the col, Zonza can be very busy, especially at lunchtime. If you have the opportunity to travel farther afield, try a detour to the nearby village of **Quenza**, which offers several good lunch stops. Alternatively, shop for local Corsican produce and have a picnic — perfect in these beautiful surroundings.

The north side of the col drops into a magnificent natural bowl blanketed with pines. The **Forêt de Bavella** (Bavella Forest) offers equally dramatic views of the mountains as those from the south, but currently the road (the D268) is being widened to allow better access and is closed intermittently. Please check with the tourist board before setting out on this route (which intersects with the N198 on the east coast at Solenzara).

THE NORTHEAST AND CAP CORSE

The northeastern section of Corsica offers many contrasts. It has been at the center of island commerce since ancient Greek times and boasts its largest town, yet also contains rural areas almost devoid of human habitation. The coastal

Bastia is home to the bustling Vieux Port and the grand church of Saint Jean Baptiste.

plains and lakes were once a rich agricultural resource and still supply oysters and mussels for local consumption, but they were also, until the mid-20th century, breeding ground for malarial mosquitoes — now thankfully eradicated — that more than once decimated surrounding towns. Today hosts of visitors return year after year to the area's sandy beaches and excellent camping grounds.

Have a good day –
Bonne journée

Bastia

Bastia is the main northeastern town, capital of Haute-Corse, and Corsica's main industrial center. In recent years the area has been almost overtaken by commercial enterprises and the working population is housed in multi-story apartment blocks. There's a hustle and bustle about the town not felt anywhere else on the island; people have things to do and places to go! At first glance this is not an inspiring destination, but Bastia has treasures to reveal.

First, head for the two parts of the Vieille Ville. The *haute ville* (high town) called Terra-Nova is a classic Genoese citadel, with high, thick walls. To the north is **Terra-Vecchia** with its tree-lined squares and fine townhouses. Between the two, **Vieux Port** (Old Harbor) is still used by the Bastia fishing fleet, and lined with old apartment blocks once inhabited by fishing families. Today the harbor hosts several restaurants and cafés where you can sit over coffee and watch the fleet at work, or listen to the locals discuss the latest political turns. Behind the harbor, a labyrinth of narrow streets offer a glimpse of everyday life in Bastia: the barbershop with its aging seats and cracked floor tiles, shoe repair shops and ships' chandlers, a seaman's mission. This area is still very much a living community.

Overlooking the harbor is the imposing façade of **Église St-Jean-Baptiste** (Church of St. John the Baptist), in Baroque style, the biggest parish church on Corsica. Nearby on Rue Napoléon are two smaller churches. The **Oratoire de l'Immaculée Conception** (Oratory of the Immaculate Conception), built in 1611, is richly decorated, with frescoes dating from the 18th century and its pillars lined with crimson damask. The church was used for the first meeting of the Anglo-Corsican Council in 1795. The statue of the Virgin Mary on display here is carried through the streets on 9 December each year. The **Oratoire de la confrérie St-Roch** is farther north, built by a grateful populace in the early 17th century to honor the saint who protected the town from a plague. It is decorated in Florentine style. West of the churches is **Place du Marché**, which still hosts a daily market. The small square is lined with houses dating from the 17th century and the old **Hôtel de Ville** or Town Hall.

On the south side of the port is an ornate set of steps leading past the formal Jardin Romieu to **Terra-Nova**. This

The Trinighellu

A small railway network running since 1888, the Trinighellu links Bastia, Calvi, Corte, and Ajaccio. This is one of the most enjoyable ways to see the island's interior without having to drive. There are several tours every day, allowing time (in theory) at each destination to explore and maybe have lunch.

It is the speed of the journey — or lack thereof — that makes the Trinighellu so much fun. As the train crawls up steep inclines and stops regularly for animals on the tracks, you'll probably have to toss out your schedule for the day, but you won't mind, as this means more time to take in the breathtaking scenery. Don't forget your camera!

citadel was in fact the new part of town when it was built by the Genoese, hence its name. **The Palias des Governeurs** (Governor's Palace) is the most striking building, with its simple 14th-century façade. Used as the Genoese court until the 18th century, the palace now houses the **Musée d'Ethnographie Corse** (Corsican Ethnology Museum). The museum is unfortunately closed until the end of 2001, as the collection is being refurbished.

Two churches lie at the southern end of the citadel. **The Église Sainte-Marie**, built in 1495, was the Episcopal seat of Corsica until this was moved to Ajaccio in 1801. The marble interior is magnificent; the ornate statue of the Virgin Mary created by Gaetano Macchi is used in the annual procession on Assumption Day. The church also displays several paintings collected by Cardinal Fesch (see page 30). Directly behind the église is **Chapelle Sainte-Croix**, which has a beautiful Baroque interior — a plethora of painted cherubs flit along the gold-leaf gilding. The black crucifix, which gives the chapel its name, is said to have been found in 1428 by fishermen in the harbor. They still offer the first catch of the new season to the cross as it is paraded through the streets on 3 May each year.

To the north of the old harbor, the streets of Bastia open out into fine boulevards laid out in the 18th and 19th centuries. Everyone seems to head for **Place Saint-Nicholas**, a 300-m- (914-ft-) long open space offering the young somewhere to play, teenagers somewhere to date, and older folks somewhere to talk about the day. Cafés and bars line the square, you'll find the Tourist Information Office here, and it is also the departure point for the *petit train* tour around the town. On Sundays the square is taken over by a huge flea market, so be prepared to spend a few francs on souvenirs.

☛ Cap Corse

North of Bastia, a finger of land 15 km (9 miles) wide sticks straight up toward the coast of mainland Italy. This is Cap Corse, buffeted by passing winds and defying the waves. A line of mountains rising to 1,307 m (4,288 ft) form a spine down its center, and apart from a road around its circumference, there are few inroads into the interior for vehicles. The buildings have a rugged quality, with roofs of slate rather than tile. The proximity of the sea and the unspoiled beauty of the place make Cap Corse a favorite for walkers, cyclists, and drivers. You can tour it in a day with a stop for lunch.

The road north out of Bastia soon leaves the town behind and, after **Miomo** with its Genoese watchtower and small beach, there are few settlements. Walking trails lead into the hills, of which **Monte Stello** is the highest; it often attracts a cloud cap.

Erbalunga comprises a wonderful collection of old buildings, which look as though they are about to fall into the sea; just north is the **Tour de Losse** (Losse Tower), one of the better-preserved Genoese towers on the island. Nearby, **Porticciolo's** pretty stone cottages surround a tiny fishing port. Finally, after 40 km (25 miles), the road makes a sharp left across the Cap at **Macinaggio**, a small settlement with a large, modern marina. To travel farther north you must put on your hiking boots and take to the footpaths. You will find deserted beaches and acres of unspoiled countryside to explore.

The road continues west, climbing through the commune of **Roglaino**, where there are a number of lovely villages. Flashes of the north coast come in and out of sight before the road reaches the opposite coast, where several abandoned windmills stand. Here, high above the waterline, is a

Tour de Losse stands high on the crags above the sea, a relic of the Genoese at Cap Corse.

tantalizing view of a small fishing port several kilometers away. **Centuri** is a narrow cove lined with small, sturdy cottages decorated with painted shutters and colorful potted plants. There are just enough restaurants around the harbor to be convenient without spoiling the atmosphere. Seafood is, naturally, the specialty, and a meal here is definitely worth the stop.

The road along the west coast continues high above the water on a path of tight, blind bends. The cliffs fall straight to the sea and the towns cling to the higher ground. At **Pino** you can climb farther into the hills for views from the **Tour de Sénèque**, which dates from the 14th century, and on up to the **Col de Santa Lucia**.

At **Marina d'Albo** the coast changes; gray slate eroded from the surrounding hills and seabed has been pounded into

The pretty Corsican village of Nonza sits high above a dramatic gray slate beach.

sand here. The most dramatic beach is at **Nonza**, which has a tiny citadel and village perched high above its wide graphite sands. A series of names marked out in white stone, the result of hard work by beachcombers, are clearly visible; less so the remains of an old seaside settlement now lost to the elements.

At the base of Cap Corse, head inland to **Patrimonio**, center of Corsican wine production, which will be obvious by the acres of vines stretching along the road. Stop at a roadside *cave* for *dégustation* (tasting) and to buy the odd bottle or two. The village church, **Église Saint-Martin**, sits atop an earth mound. It dates from 1510, but was restored in the early 19th century. Set in its shadow is a **menhir** dating from the first century B.C., which was found in a vineyard in the valley in 1964.

At the base of Cap Corse along the coast is the town of **Saint-Florent**, called simply Saint Flo by Corsicans. A 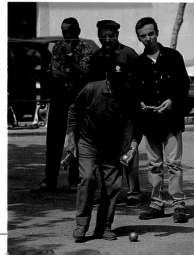 delightful fishing port, it is now one of the fastest growing resorts on the island. The nearby mouth of the Aliso River is full of local craft, and a new marina welcomes yachts and sailboats during the season. The old town surrounds a small citadel; its dungeon (*donjon*) is in the process of renovation, but there is little else in the interior. A delightful promenade with cafés and chic boutiques traverses the seafront, and there is a sandy beach just around the bay. Saint-Florent was the site of the first Pisan bishopric dating from 1077, and the **Cathedral of Nebbio**, lying 700 m (¹/₂ mile) from the center of town, was once the most important church on the island. Inside is the mummified remains of St. Flor, the Roman soldier martyred for his faith in the third century A.D. who gave his name to the town.

Saint-Florent is the capital of the Nebbio region, which lies in the hills between here and Bastia to the east. It is an area of windswept, rolling hills blanketed with pastureland filled with cattle ranches. In Genoese times it was known as the "golden shell" of Corsica, for the corn crops that were grown here. A few villages lie on the D162 road, which cuts across the region. Pride of the Nebbio is **Église**

Local men play pétanque in the town square — perhaps they'll let you pitch a few.

Visitors are drawn to the multi-colored façade of the church of Saint Michel.

Saint Michel, on this road at Murato. In a splendid spot on a grassy knoll, this beautiful Pisan church is constructed of a pale limestone and green marble, giving its façade a checkerboard effect. Decorated with animal heads and gargoyles, it warrants close inspection. Local people say that a mosque stood here during the time of the Moors and the grotesque carvings celebrate the Christian victory and Pisan possession of the island.

If you are returning to Bastia from Murato, take the route known as the **Défilé de Lancôme**, the narrowest of roads through a deep ravine. The passage is probably more fun for the passenger than the driver, but the view is very impressive!

East of Saint-Florent is an area known as the **Désert des Agriates**, now a barren wilderness but once a fertile wheat-growing region and shepherding pasture. There are no towns here, and the one main road is not well surfaced. But the beaches surrounding the area are spectacular, and, since most can only be reached by footpath or boat from Saint-Florent, relatively unspoiled. There are no facilities, so take refreshment and always remember to carry your trash out with you.

South from Bastia

The route south from Bastia is probably the least inspiring area of Corsica. For almost 20 km (12 miles) the view from the main road is of only the industrial and commercial estates of the suburbs. Avoid this by taking the narrow coast road to the east; it passes the long beaches of Bastia and Biguglia and the **Étang de Biguglia**, a natural reserve for wetland birds and animals. This road can be very busy on weekends, crowded with local families heading out for the day.

South of the étang is the remains of the second Roman settlement on Corsica, **Mariana**. Gaius Marius founded the town around 100 B.C., but it never rivaled Aléria farther south. It was destroyed in the fifth century and silt covered its remains. Today, an old street and the foundations of a fourth-century basilica and baptistery can be seen. The cathedral, **La Canonica**, which was the seat of the Bishopric of Corsica after the Cathedral at Saint-Florent, dates from 1119 but was built on fourth-century Roman foundations. Constructed of alternate layers of light and dark stone, in Corsican-Pisan style, it is decorated with a simple animal frieze on the door lintel. Another earlier church nearby, **San Perteo**, is smaller and simpler in design. The cemetery here has been excavated, revealing burials from pre-Christian times to the medieval era.

Just below La Canonica, the main route splits from the N193, heading west toward Corte. The road follows the path of the **Golo River**, which is a favorite with kayakers and canoeists. Look out for an old bridge on your right at the river crossing at **Ponte Nouvo**. A Corsican Moor's-head flag marks the spot where French troops beat a battle-weary Corsican army and finally won control of the island.

Crossing the Genoese bridge at **Ponte Leccia**, the road splits again, with a route to Calvi and l'Île Rousse to the right (see page 68). Take time to examine the architectural details of the bridge, which is in excellent condition and still used as the main highway. As you travel south, take a short detour to **Castirla**; its 15th-century **Chapelle San Michel** is decorated with beautiful frescoes.

☛ Corte

Another 30 km (18 miles) brings you to **Corte**, distinguished by its medieval citadel looming high above the modern town. Set in a bowl surrounded by the highest peaks on Corsica, Corte is the geographical center of the island. The heartland of nationalism during the 18th century, it was the seat of the Corsican government during its short period of independence. The town was fought over by many of Corsica's heroes; Corso took it in 1553 and General Gaffori in 1746. During early French rule the town fell into decline and its geographical position, compared to the coastal locations, put it at a disadvantage. Since the re-opening of the University de la Corse in 1981, however, Corte has taken on a new vibrancy.

Corte's new town has spread along the valley floor, but the old town is a compact area of cobbled streets lined with cafés and shops selling pottery or wooden souvenirs. At the base of the old town, **Place Paoli** boasts a bronze statue of the man himself; he's facing down **Cours Paoli**, the main shopping boulevard. Head up the steep flight of steps leading from Cours Paoli to a smaller square featuring an ornate fountain with four cannons in its design. The fountain once had more than a decorative function, providing fresh water for the military garrison in the citadel above. You will find the Tourist Information Office here.

Another set of steps from Place Paoli lead up to **Place Gaffori** in the heart of the old town. Here a statue of the square's namesake points the way to the citadel, as if urging his troops on. Behind the statue is the Gaffori house, to which the Genoese laid siege in 1750. Though the enemy kidnapped his son, General Gaffori refused to yield; his wife Faustina threatened to blow up the building herself rather than let the Genoese take it. Bullet holes from the battle are still visible on the walls.

Climb higher yet to reach the citadel, passing the house of the Casanova family on your right. The former residents were relatives of the Bonaparte family, who stayed here while Bonaparte Sr. fought alongside Paoli. In fact, Napoléon's older brother Joseph was born here, before the family moved to Ajaccio.

Steep medieval streets wind their way through the old town section of Corte.

On the left is the **Palais National**, where the Corsican government met between 1755–1769. It now houses the university faculty of Corsican Studies.

Just through the main gate of the **citadel** is a rather unremarkable open space lined with 19th-century barracks. Occupied by the Foreign Legion from 1963 until 1983, today its halls are used as university faculty housing. At the far edge of the square is the entrance to the **Musée de la Corse**.

The museum is an interesting fusion of ancient and modern. Housed in the former Sérurier Barracks, the space has been redesigned to offer a state-of-the-art area for temporary art and design exhibitions, plus an ethnology section exhibiting displays about different facets of the traditional Corsican lifestyle. Here you can learn about chestnut farming, shepherding, Corsican craftsmanship, and religious brotherhoods — all of which still exist on the island. Using artifacts and oral anecdotes, this exhibition brings the recent past to life. There is multi-lingual accompaniment to allow a greater understanding of each area's significance.

Through the museum are the inner walls of the citadel and the steep steps up to the **Eagle's Nest** (*nid d'aigle*), a tiny cas-

tle sitting at the very pinnacle of the citadel atop a rock platform. Created in the 1420s by Vincentello d'Istria for the Aragonese crown, it is the only inland citadel on the island. Aside from the opportunity to peer into the old dungeons and explore the small watchtowers, this place is worth a visit for the spectacular view across the surrounding valleys to the mountains beyond. Make your way south around the outer walls of the lower citadel to

Corte's regal citadel is the only one in Corsica not located near the seaside.

Wild pigs and piglets are a common sight throughout Corsica — use caution when driving on country roads.

the belvedere, a small viewing platform, for another excellent vista including the citadel itself.

The mountains surrounding Corte offer wonderful opportunities for walking and hiking. Explore the forests along the **Gorges du Tavignano** to the west, or the neighboring **Gorge de la Restonica**, where a narrow road allows vehicle access. It is possible to reach the impressive lakes of **Monte Rotondo** at heights of over 1,500 m (4,572 ft), from the end of the road.

South of Corte, the spectacular **Col de Vizzavona** carries the main road toward Ajaccio. The village of **Bocognano** still produces flour in its old chestnut mill. The high peaks and pine forest here make for an impressive sight. **Monte**

Archaeologists have made great strides in uncovering the ancient Greek and Roman history of Corsica.

Renoso, 2,353 m (7,720 ft) high, has a winter-sports station on its northern flank.

South along the Coast

Heading south from the intersection with the N193, the N198 leads along a coastal plain filled with vines and fruit trees and dotted with small coastal resorts — all recent additions and not particularly inspiring. A long strip of sand attracts many visitors, but there is relatively little to hold the touring visitor save a few vineyards offering *dégustation*. Inland, however, is one of Corsica's most interesting regions, the **Castagniccia**. This is the heartland of chestnut production and is still filled with traditional rural villages.

Take the D506 into the hills and you will begin to see a change as you climb. Chestnut forests to blanket the slopes along with cork oaks, their trunks stripped of bark and painted to prevent infection. Underneath the trees are nets either laid out or neatly folded. These catch the harvested chestnuts as they fall. At almost every turn there are pig corrals for pigs, or families of the creatures trotting along the roadside on their way to forage the forest floor for fallen chestnuts, roots, and leaves. Abundant fresh streams keep them supplied with water, and mud to bathe in.

The villages of the Castagniccia are rugged and sturdy — their buildings are functional rather than beautiful — but they do have a pleasing aspect, sitting as they do on high ridges between densely forested vales. Pascal Paoli was born in this region, at Stretta, a small settlement in the commune of **Morosaglia**. His birthplace has been converted into a small museum and his tomb can be viewed in the small chapel next door. His body was returned here in 1889, from England, where he died in exile in 1807.

Return to the east coast by taking the D71 past the villages of **Ortale** and **Cervione**. It's then only 24 km (15 miles) to the old Greek and Roman capital of Corsica, **Aléria**. Thoughtfully sited on high ground above the Tavignano River, this area, with a small cluster of houses around a small main square, is still occupied in the present day. The actual archaeological site displays vestiges of walls and the remains of columns left after barbarians destroyed the city in the fourth century A.D.. The attached museum offers more interesting insight into the lives of the people who occupied the city. **Musée Jérôme Carcopino** occupies the Genoese **Fort Mantra**, which has been fully restored. It was here that "King Théodore of Corsica" held court in 1736, before abandoning his claim when French troops arrived to reinforce Genoese sovereignty. The museum displays finds from all eras of ancient Aléria, a veritable treasure-trove of objects from the mundane to the elaborate. Hairpins and sewing needles, soup ladles and cooking pots of the later Roman period contrast with the richly decorated pottery found in Greek tombs at the site. This Greek pottery, dating from the fifth and fourth centuries B.C., is especially exquisite; two animal-head flagons attributed to the artist Byrgos have an almost lifelike quality. Other objects depict the gods of classical Greece, such as Pan playing his pipes. Many of these objects originated from the Italian and Greek mainland and also from the African coast.

THE NORTHWEST

The northwest region of Corsica offers a spectacular range of natural attractions. The highest peak on the island, Monte Cinto, sits inland, and Scandola, an UNESCO site, occupies a finger of land on the western coast. Genoese fortifications dot the coastline and artisan villages rest in the foothills. This area also has the most cosmopolitan resort on the island, making a luxurious base from which to explore.

☞ Calvi

The town of Calvi occupies a commanding position at the southwestern point of a wide sandy bay. Promoting itself as a seaside retreat since the 1840s, it was fashionable long before the Côte d'Azur, across the water in France, ever was. Local legend has it that Christopher Columbus was born here, as he was of Genoese origin, but several towns in Italy make the same claim. Italians, along with just about every other nationality, still flock here in the thousands, to sit by the elegant marina and sip an apéritif before dinner, or to stroll among the yachts in the harbor and chat with their skippers.

Greeks and Roman settled the surrounding area but evidence of their settlements was destroyed in barbarian raids. When the Genoese arrived in the 13th century Calvi was a simple fishing village, but they saw strategic advantage in its location and set about building their citadel overlooking the approach to the bay. Calvi stood strong against Corsican freedom fighters throughout the struggles, and after the French takeover of the island, during the period of the Anglo/Corsican Council, it was bombarded by forces loyal to Paoli but did not capitulate.

Today the **citadel** is still an impressive sight; its walls have been constantly maintained. A stroll around the narrow cobbled streets reveals few concessions to tourism, just a couple of restaurants scattered among family homes — perhaps this citadel more than any other on Corsica offers an impression of how the Genoese once lived. The striking **Genoese Governor's Palace**, built in the 13th century, is now used by the French Foreign Legion, which has a large base on the plain across the bay — uniformed soldiers still stroll

Calvi has been a popular seaside destination for more than 150 years.

through the streets. The major church, **Église St. Jean-Baptiste** (St. John the Baptist), was founded in the 13th century but badly damaged by a gunpowder explosion in the garrison in 1567. The Renaissance-style baptismal font near the main entrance was given to the church in 1569 to mark the completion of its renovation.

The town of Calvi sits outside the walls around a small **port**. This is where the action is, with shops filling the narrow streets and café/bars along the water's edge. Boats along the dockside offer day-trips to the Scandola Reserve and Girolata. Once the main shopping street, **Rue Clemenceau** is now a pedestrian walkway (*rue piétonne*) with a good selection of clothing boutiques, souvenir stores, and restaurants. On a small square off Rue Clemenceau is **Église Ste-Marie-Majeure**, a pretty church with its small dome, campanile, and rose-and-ochre façade. The church was built on the site of a fourth-century paleo-Christian place of worship destroyed in barbarian raids. Recitals are held here in the summer months.

Rue Clemenceau becomes Rue Joffre as you move south, and this leads to the main tourist information center and to the train station for routes along the coast and to Bastia or Corte.

Farther along around the bay, you will find the main beach, a long arc of sand well equipped with restaurants and watersports stations.

North from Calvi

North of Calvi are occasional settlements set in the sandy bays — these bustle in the summer as campgrounds fill up for the season. A local train service along the coast from Calvi links these resorts and offers a relaxing way to travel. Its northernmost stop is at **L'Île-Rousse**, a pretty town, interesting actually for its lack of a Genoese citadel. When Paoli came to power the Genoese occupied many coastal towns, but he needed a coastal port for trade and supplies; he founded L'Île-Rousse for this purpose in 1758. Although he attempted to build a protective tower, it never matched the might of his rivals — the tower is now encircled with elegant mansions.

The heart of the town is Place Paoli; its colonnaded marketplace hosts a morning fish market. *Boules* players pit their skills during regular afternoon matches in the tree-lined square, which is graced by a marble statue of Paoli. There is a small **aquarium**

Time-honored traditions — such as the hand-mending of fishing nets — prevail here.

in the port featuring local Mediterranean sea life. The seafront is traversed by a modern promenade leading to some good sandy beaches. The sea here remains shallow for 30 m (98 ft), making it a perfect spot for young children, but the beaches get busy in high season. Head north toward Lozari for quieter locations.

High in the hills above L'Île-Rousse and Calvi, in what is known as the **Balagne** region, are a series of small villages. Take the D151 from the west or the N197 from the east to

The Balagne region is home to a host of small villages and rustic churches.

enjoy a circular tour through them on a road called **Route des Artisans**, or Strada di l'Artigiani, named for the many artisans who have set up workshops in the region. Unlike the villages of the tree-filled Castagniccia, the elegant Balagne villages can be easily viewed from far across the low-growing *macchia*. The northernmost villages are **Belgodère** and **Palasca**; from here the road hugs the hillside, traveling past small olive groves, the settlements strung out like pearls on a necklace. Turn up the hill to reach **Speloncato** for a quick jog through before returning to the original route. Once you reach **Cateri** head toward Aregno, but don't miss a visit to **Sant' Antonino**, high on a rocky rise. The village, looking almost like an eagle's nest from a distance, is a maze of cobbled streets with several fine restaurants perfect for a lunch stop.

Aregno has one of the finest Pisan churches on the island. **Église de la Trinité** sits in a village graveyard filled with family tombs of white marble decorated with fresh flowers. The stunning exterior of red and mustard granite is decorated with naïve figures and grotesque demons, the interior with fine frescoes dating from the 15th century.

Parc Naturel Régional de la Corse

This huge natural area, covering over 350,000 hectares (864,850 acres), was created in 1972. It stretches across the island, encompassing most of the high central mountains along with four coastal areas: Cargèse, Porto, and Galéria on the west coast, and Migliacciaru in the east. The mission of the park authorities is first to protect the animals and plants native to the landscape. These include eagles, mouflon (a species of wild mountain sheep), and the cerf (a type of deer), which has been reintroduced into the region following its near extinction through hunting. Second, the park preserves traditional buildings, and controls future development, including support of village communities and renovation of isolated farmhouses and churches. The authorities also undertake to educate the local population about the park and its activities, and allows public access through footpath development and controlled sporting and outdoor activities. Finally, it must ensure an environmental balance in all activities.

The control of activities versus access is perhaps the biggest issue facing the park. However, refuges have been created on the walking trails. This is most obvious on the GR20 hiking route, where well-signposted paths mean hikers are clear about routes so footfall damage is kept to a minimum, and there are areas marked out for camping so true lovers of the area can stay overnight.

More information can be found on the park web site at <www.parc-naturel-corse.com>.

Nearby is the village of **Pigna**, famed for its population of artisans. This tiny village is home to potters, instrument makers, and artists, and is also a center for traditional Corsican music.

The largest and most southerly artisanal town in the Balagne is **Calezana**, reached from Calvi via the road to Ste-Catherine Airport. This is also the starting point for the famed GR20 hiking route, which leads hikers over the highest peaks on Corsica. Monte Cinto and the other mountains of the Monte Grosso region can be seen here, rising to frame the Bay of Calvi and the Balagne region. To reach the area by car take the D47 road from the interior through the **Gorges de Asco** to the winter and summer sports station of **Haut Asco**.

South from Calvi

The area south of Calvi is relatively unpopulated until you reach the town of **Galéria** (via the D81 or D81b), historically a center of cheese production because the surrounding land provided winter grazing for large flocks of sheep, which were taken to higher mountain pastures during the summer. Today flocks are smaller and the long hikes to summer pasture have been replaced by truck journeys — even the sheep get to ride. Galéria is now attracting visitors in larger numbers as the jumping-off point for the **Réserve Naturelle de Scandola** (Scandola Natural Reserve) to the south. Covering 919 hectares (2,271 acres) of land and 1,000 hectares (2,471 acres) of marine environment, Scandola, created in 1975, was awarded UNESCO world heritage status in 1983. The site, characterized by huge volcanic rock formations, protects many rare species, including eagles and puffins. There is no road access, preserving the peace and quiet as well as the environment. The one settlement within the park, **Girolata**, can be reached by boat from Galéria in the north or Porto in the south (journeys take approximately one hour). There are a couple of restaurants here; after lunch put on your hiking boots and explore this wild and rugged area.

South of Galéria, the road leads inland, skirting the **Forêt du Fangu** on the left, until it begins to wind down to the small resort of **Porto**. Set in the gorge of the Porto River, this town boasts a pretty Genoese tower overlooking the sea. Several restaurants fan out along the seafront, making Porto a popular place to stop for lunch — try to get here a little before noon to beat the tour buses. Porto gets very busy in season, as it stands at the crossing of two major tourist routes

The rugged rock of Les Calanches along the coast is an awe-inspiring sight — have your camera at the ready.

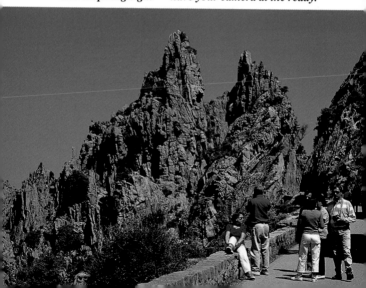

and provides access to the Scandola Reserve, along with offering a natural stopping place on trips north from Ajaccio or south from Calvi.

Carry on south on the D81 along the coast, which is lined with some of the most beautiful and spectacular landscape on Corsica. **Les Calanches** is a stretch of rose-red rock carved into spectacular shapes by millennia of wind and water erosion. The road twists

> **Have a good evening –**
> *Bonne soirée*

and turns through magnificent vistas of rock and pine forest for 11 km (7 miles). You'll need to stop often, as many abandon their vehicles along the road for a photo opportunity — but fortunately everyone has to drive so slowly here that the ride isn't too unnerving. At the end of les Calanches is the small village of **Piana**, from where there are beautiful views across the bay to the Scandola Reserve in the distance.

Continue south on the road to Ajaccio to reach **Cargèse**. In 1670 Corsica saw an influx of Greek settlers who, having been forced to leave their homes because of Ottoman Turk invasion, sought the protection of their Genoese allies. They moved to various locations before, in 1773, they finally settled in Cargèse, building a Greek Orthodox church on a hillside facing the Catholic church. Built in 1852, the Greek church contains religious icons completely different in character to the trompe-l'oeil decorative art of the Latin church. Both communities vie to produce the most impressive religious procession on their respective feast days. The town itself is relatively modern, and offers some interesting souvenir stores.

The route inland from Porto leads into the heart of the Parc Naturel Régional de la Corse (see page 45) in a most dramatic fashion. The D84 begins to climb almost immediately after Porto; within a few kilometers it has risen above the tree line and climbs along the side of the vertiginous **Gorge de Spelunca**. The village of **Ota** sits across the gorge on the path of the Mare e Monte hiking route; footpath and road converge at **Evisa** higher in the hills. From here there are many shorter walks to choose from, including access down into the gorge itself.

Passing over the **Col de Vergio**, the highest on Corsica at 1,477 m (4,846 ft), you'll see the chairlifts used to service the winter *pistes* (ski runs) before dropping down through the pine forest to the **Niolo Basin**. One of the most remote locations on the island until recent times — the road was completed at the end of the 19th century — it sits in the shadow of Monte Cinto, the highest on the island. The basin was once the summer feeding ground for huge herds of goats and sheep and continues to be the shepherds' domain. There are no towns, only mountains, streams, and lots of fresh air; since access has been improved, the forests around here have become a favorite place for Corsicans to escape the heat of long summer days. Although the shepherding tradition is in decline, the Niolo still holds its yearly festival in the first week of September, which has always marked the change of season and the beginning of preparations to come down from the high plains to the winter feeding grounds.

The route out at the northern end of the valley is no less dramatic than the Gorge de Spelunca. Here the young Golo River has eroded a deep, narrow ravine called the **Scala de Santa Regina**. Somehow engineers have managed to create a a 15-km (9-mile) road through the ravine; in some places it seems to defy gravity. Alongside is the old, narrow donkey track that was once the only route to Corte from here.

Corsica Highlights

Musée Fesch. 50-52 Rue de Cardinal Fesch, 20000 Ajaccio; Tel. 04 95 21 48 17. Gallery with fine collection of European art. Open summer Tue–Sun 9am–noon, 3pm–7pm, Fridays July–August 9pm–midnight; winter Tue–Sat 9am–noon, 2:30pm–6pm. Admission fee.

Musée National de la Maison Bonaparte. Rue Saint-Charles, 20000 Ajaccio; Tel. 04 95 21 43 89. The birthplace and childhood home of Napoléon Bonaparte. Open 9am– noon, 2pm–6pm; 1 Oct–20 Jun 10am–noon, 2pm–5pm. Closed Sunday afternoon and Monday morning. Admission fee.

Musée Départemental de Jérôme Carcopino. 20270 Aléria; Tel. 04 95 57 00 92. Archaeological site dating back to the Neolithic period. Open 8am–noon, 2pm–7pm; 1 Oct–15 May 8am–noon, 2pm–5pm. Closed 1 Jan, 1 May, 11 Nov. Admission fee.

Musée Départemental de Levie. Hôtel de Ville, 20170 Levie; Tel. 04 95 78 46 34; fax 04 95 78 41 60. Archaeological finds including the 6000-year-old skeleton "La Dame de Bonifacio." Open daily July–15 Sept 10am–6pm; May–June Mon–Sat 10am–noon, 2pm–4:30pm; 16 Sept–30 Apr Tue–Sat 10am–noon, 2pm–4:40pm. Admission fee.

Musée Départemental de Préhistoire Corse. 20100 Sartene; Tel. 04 95 77 01 09. Collection explaining and illustrating the evolution of human development and settlement on Corsica. Open Mon–Sat 10am–noon, 2pm–6pm; 16 Sept–14 June Mon–Fri 10am–noon, 2pm–5pm. Admission fee.

Filitosa. Commune de Filitosa; Tel. 04 95 74 00 91. Megalithic and torréen site. Open daily 1 Apr–31 Oct 8am–sunset. Admission fee.

Le Musée de la Corse. La Citadelle, 20250 Corte; Tel. 04 95 45 25 45; fax 04 95 45 25 36; web site <www.sitec.fr/ museu>. Collections relating to Corsican lifestyle and traditions, also entrance to the historic citadel of the city. Open daily 22 June–20 Sept 10am–8pm; 21 Sept–31 Oct Tues–Sun 10am–6pm; 1 Nov–31 Mar Tue–Sat 10am–6pm; 1 Apr–21 June Tue–Sun 10am– 6pm. Admission fee.

WHAT TO DO

Corsica, with its acres of forest, numerous rivers, mountain peaks, sandy beaches, and clear seas, is heaven for those who love the outdoors. Add to this lots of fresh air (there is little heavy industry on the island) and a temperate climate, and the island has an abundance of raw material to feed the sportsman's fantasies. There is a well-organized infrastructure for recreation on the island, with professional instructors and modern equipment available. There are numerous participation sports and activities offered for all interests and fitness levels.

For those who don't want to break into a sweat on vacation, Corsica has the perfect solution; let someone else take the strain and enjoy a number of organized events which won't make the heart race with anything other than excitement and wonder.

Many of the following activities are seasonal; the season starts on 1 May and ends on 1 October (high season is between 15 July and the end of August). Outside of these dates many activities are limited, so do confirm your arrangements before traveling.

SPORT

On Land

Walking and hiking. Corsica is the perfect island for these activities which the French call *randonnée*. The national park and coastal areas are crisscrossed with footpaths on routes which can take a few hours or many days. *Grandes Randonnées*, or long distance routes (shortened to GR), and *Petites Randonnées* (PR) are well signposted every 50 m (165 ft) or so and take you through some of the island's loveliest scenery.

The most famous of these is the GR20 — known locally as the Fra I Monti — considered one of the best and most challenging in France. The route travels northwest/southeast across the island over the highest peaks of the interior; the whole trek takes 15 days. A series of mountain refuges for overnight accommodation have been built along the route, and camping is allowed around these sites.

On the higher routes, hiking is best undertaken after mid-May, when the snow has melted. In spring the routes are awash with wildflowers, including several species found only on Corsica and Sardinia. Don't forget to take water and calories in some form, along with a layer of warm clothing just in case the weather changes quickly.

While the longest and most remote paths require a high level of fitness and experience with mountain terrain, the *Office National des Fôrets* on Corsica have also created a number of shorter "discovery" walks through areas of particular significance or importance. These are both entertaining and educational, and open to people of average fitness levels. A booklet explaining the different routes is available from Maison d'Information du Parc Naturel Régional, 2, rue Sergent Casalongo, B.P. 417, 20184 Ajaccio, cedex France; Tel. 04 95 51 79 00; fax 04 95 21 88 17; web site <www.parc-naturel-corse.com>. There is a small charge for leaflets and booklets.

For those who simply want to stroll, the cliffs east of Bonifacio offer easy routes with superb views over the citadel. You can walk 8 km (5 miles) to the end of the Golfe de Sperono and the scant remains of a Roman villa, or take a small boat to the Iles Lavezza just offshore. Or walk between the three megalithic sites at Cauria; the route is flat and the journey takes about 30 minutes, plus additional time to explore the sites.

Cycling. The French have always been at the forefront of this sport, and there are road routes to follow either as part of a group or alone. The mountains offer some particularly challenging ascents, but for those with enough stamina, the reward is in the extraordinary views. The newer sport of mountain biking can be enjoyed along the many footpaths, bridleways, and woodland trails. You can rent a bike when you arrive and join a group on a pre-set itinerary, or set out and explore the well-marked paths in the area yourself.

Corsica boasts a variety of outdoor sports for the more adventurous traveler.

If you'd like to join a walking or cycling tour but don't want to camp or carry your luggage everywhere, there are several companies who will organize your itinerary and transport your luggage so that it is waiting when you arrive at the next hotel at the end of the day.

Horseback riding. The island offers 1,900 km (1,180 miles) of bridleways for what the French call *randonnée équestre*. You can take horseback-riding classes or rent a horse and take to the hills in supervised groups. This is a great way to explore the countryside, either along the coastal plains of the east or through the forests. Most stables will advertise at roadside — often with the word "ranch" or a picture of a horse.

*Don't worry about the kids — children can be kept busy
with activities from kayaking to horseback riding!*

Parapente. The French invented the *parapente*, or air wing,
a type of navigable parachute. You'll probably see individu-
als in the air, soaring above the hillsides. There are a number
of places to take instruction or a flight in tandem with an
instructor. Hang-gliding is also available.

Climbing. There are thirty official climbing sites in Corsica
with qualified instructors or supervisors and equipment for
sale or rent. Even beginners can try their hand in relative
safety at these locations. Of course there are many other
unsupervised sites for those with experience and confidence.
With several mountain peaks rising to over 1,500 m (4,500
ft), Corsica offers many challenges to all ability levels.

Winter sports. The national park supports three winter
resorts for downhill (*alpin*) and cross-country (*ski de fond*)
skiing. The season lasts more or less from December

through April. The largest resort can be found south of Calvi at Aso, but there are also several runs at Vergio at the summit of the Spelunca Gorge. Cross-country skiing is available at the Plateau de Cuscione in the south.

On the Water

Boat rental and sailing. Ports all around the island have boats for rent, ranging from small rowboats to large pleasure cruisers. With a bit of instruction you will soon be free to take out a small boat to explore and snorkel in little coves, or find yourself a secluded bay for sunbathing. Alternatively, take a day sail (or longer) with meals and captain included; all you have to do is relax and enjoy the sea air. The many ports along Corsica's 1,000-km (600-mile) coastline are well equipped and make great bases for stepping off to explore dry land.

Canoe/kayak/rafting. Watercourses on the island include rapids, gorges, waterfalls, and pools fed by melt water and spring rainfall, but there is also a well-developed sea kayaking circuit for visitors to enjoy. The water table remains high until relatively late in the season, which means safer conditions for beginners. Canoeing and white-water rafting are best from March until early June.

Hunting

Hunting is a traditional activity on Corsica, where wild animals are seen as a welcome supplement to a mostly vegetable diet. It is still very popular, with most rural homes possessing a shotgun. There are different shooting seasons for various types of animals, though not in the protected parks and reserves. When touring by car or on foot watch out for signs with the words *Réserve pour la Chasse*, or *Chasse Guarde;* these indicate that you are in an area where hunting takes place. And if you see groups of men with shotguns, don't be alarmed!

Canyoning and spelunking. Swimming through gorges and caves are both becoming more popular and are best undertaken in high water levels.

Diving and snorkeling. The coastline of Corsica offers excellent dive sites, and there are over 30 dive clubs which offer instruction and training, supervision, and equipment rental. Corsica has two sea parks: *Le Parc Marin de Corse* lies just south of Calvi in the Gulf of Porto, and *Le Parc Marin International des Bouches de Bonifacio* covers an area off the southeast coast.

Beach activities. Some people come to Corsica just to relax and take in the sun. The best beaches are along the east coast of the island; they are well-equipped with refreshments for visitors. The coastal resorts also offer the usual excitements: water skiing, jet-skiing, windsurfing, and inflatable rides. Be aware that nude bathing (*naturisme*) is allowed on some beaches, and that topless bathing is standard practice all over the island.

You need to check the small print in your insurance if you'd like to take part in some of the activities listed above. Insurance companies regard some of these, such as canyoning and jet-skiing, as dangerous or extreme sports, which may mean that you'll need to take out extra coverage if you wish to partake.

A comprehensive list of the associations governing each sport and companies providing activities can be obtained from the Agence du Tourisme de la Corse, 17 Boulevard Roi-Jérôme, 2000 Ajaccio; Tel. 04 95 51 77 77; fax 04 95 51 14 40; web site <www.corsica-online.com>.

ENTERTAINMENT

Sea excursions. All the main towns offer boat trips, called *promenade en mer* in French, which can last from a half hour

*View the island from aboard a tourist cruiser, or take a
ferry to nearby Italy for a day of sight-seeing.*

to a whole day depending on your location. Porto and
Galéria on the west coast offer trips to the Scandola Natural
Park, a UNESCO site; the only settlement here is Girolata, a
village with no road access. You can explore the beautiful
pine forests free from the noise of the 21st century.

From Bonifacio you can travel along the coastline to find
caves and cliffs, and of course get a wonderful view of the
citadel. In summer there are journeys to the Iles Lavazzi a
little way offshore. It is also possible to take a day trip to
Sardinia, 20 km (12 miles) away (one hour by ferry) to
explore the little port of Santa-Teresa-Gallura and get a taste
of Italy for the day.

Sightseeing flights. Corsica looks beautiful from the air,
where one can truly appreciate the amazing contrasts that the
island has to offer. Corse Hélicoptère offers helicopter

tours — they are located at the airport at Ajaccio; Tel. 04 95 22 77 07; fax 04 95 20 84 18.

Train journeys. The Trinighallu is Corsica's idiosyncratic train service, which travels though some of the most impressive landscape in the north of the island. A train journey is a great option for those who really don't want to drive through the often narrow roads of the interior. There are two trips per day linking Bastia, Calvi, and Corte with stops along the way. During the summer there are several trips a day linking Calvi and Ille Rousse with the smaller resorts along this coast.

Petits trains (small motorized sightseeing vehicles) operate in Ajaccio, Bonifacio, Corte, Ile Rousse, and Porto-Vecchio. The guided tours last around 20–30 minutes. In Bonifacio the petit train is a popular way to reach the citadel from the port, around 60 m (200 ft) below.

The petits trains that run in many towns are a fun way to get around — without having to climb all those steep hills!

Nightlife

Corsica's nightlife is limited compared with some other Mediterranean islands. For most people a good dinner and a glass of wine is followed by a stroll around the harbor or the town square, where the local people sit and chat about the day, or, more likely, politics.

The main resorts have discotheques or clubs. These are open every night in high season — and the local young people enjoy this as much as the visitors — but out of season they operate only on weekends, if at all. Ajaccio has a casino with roulette, blackjack, and gaming machines, called *machines à sous* in French.

SHOPPING

The tradition of self-sufficiency on Corsica has led to the development of a number of small-scale workshops which produce beautiful and practical articles, often completely hand-made. These are now the basis of souvenir shopping opportunities on the island.

Casa di l'Artigiani are shops run by CORSICADA, an organization set up to promote the work of Corsican artisans and craftspeople. They sell only high-quality goods produced on the island and offer different traditional goods in one location. Casa di l'Artigiani stores can be found in Ajaccio, Bastia, Bonifacio, Cargèse, Corte Muato, Pigna, Sartène, and Zonza.

Corsican Polyphony

Traditional musical forms are enjoying a renaissance in Corsica, particularly the a *capella* (unaccompanied voice) *paghjelle* style of the countryside. The laments, for one or several voices, tell of the hard island life, lost love, or family feuds. Several music festivals feature this form of music, which is sung only by men.

Find the perfect souvenir at the street market on Boulevard Pascal Rossini.

Pottery. Traditionally used for storage of liquids and other foodstuffs. Today you can buy practical articles such as plates, jugs, and urns, or beautiful display pieces decorated with a range of traditional glazes or Greek or Roman patterns.

Basketware. Baskets come in a range of sizes, from tabletop bread baskets to laundry carriers or log storage for beside the fireplace. They are beautifully crafted from a range of local materials such as reeds and grasses.

Wood and bone. The forest that blankets the island interior offers incomperable raw materials. Cork, used to make placemats and coasters, has been a traditional resource for centuries. Wood from the chestnut tree (*châtaigne*), used to make pipes in days gone by, is still worked into designs. Olive wood is quite beautiful, being highly grained; it is used to make bowls in a range of sizes and salad servers, among other items. Walking sticks are also popular; many make great decorative pieces in addition to being practical. Bone is often used in the design of the handle — the shepherds would often spend long hours out on the hillsides, amusing themselves by shaping goat horn or boar tusk into decorative pieces.

Traditional knife handles are also made of bone. These knives can be found in stores all across the island. They are still used in hunting — they were also used once in Corsican vendettas — but now make practical souvenirs for campers, hikers, and sailors.

Coral and shell. Most often these are fashioned into exquisite beaded necklaces, earrings, rings, and broaches, which can range in color from pale as mother of pearl to vivid red. The harvesting of coral is tightly controlled and licenses are only granted to a small number of divers. Stores selling coral pieces will advertise outside with the French word *corail*.

Boutiques. Shops selling beachwear and clothing can be found in the main towns. The clothes are influenced by both Italian and French design, so whatever you purchase will probably be quite chic.

Edibles. Local farmers once preserved foods to make the most of the harvests and to keep them though the winters. Preserved foods are still an important part of the local diet; they also make delicious souvenirs — imagine enjoying a Corsican picnic on your return home. Whole olives and delicious virgin olive oil can be found in abundance, along with fragrant honey from the *macchia* pollen.

A colorful acquisition found in some Corsican shops is striking coral beadwork.

A delicatessen features a variety of cured meats and other local favorites.

Honey produced during different seasons tastes different — summer honey is unlike that harvested in the spring. Of the range of flavors on offer, mint honey is a local specialty and has a very particular taste. Local jams are delicious, packed with fruit. Fruit is also preserved in juice or alcohol — chestnuts and figs prepared this way are a favorite with the Corsicans.

If you visit one of the *fermes auberges* (farms which sell their own produce and perhaps meals as well) or a food market, you can buy preserved meats, smoked hams, patés, and sausages — delicious with the local bread. The pork meat is flavored by the chestnut diet on which the pigs are fed. Meat from hunted wild pigs or boars takes on the flavor of wild herbs, offering a different taste sensation. Finally, do not neglect to take home a bottle of fruit-flavored *eau-de-vie,* or Cap Corse liqueur in a bottle the shape of the island with a portrait of Napoléon on the label for that extra Corsican touch.

ACTIVITIES FOR CHILDREN

If you are bringing active older children and are worried about keeping them busy, never fear — your only concern will be keeping up with them.

The beach is perfect for kids of all ages (and the adults they have in tow). Little ones can play in the sand and paddle in the calm water. Both Calvi and l'Île Rousse have excellent beaches for young children. The west coast offers

> When entering a shop, always say hello – *bonjour Madame/Monsieur*; when leaving, say thank you and goodbye – *merci, au revoir*.

opportunities for snorkeling along the rocky headlands, which older children may find more entertaining. Palombaggio boasts, perhaps, the best of both worlds, along with acres of wild-scrub–covered sand dunes crawling with lots of lizards and bird life. The range of watersports on offer should please all older children. They can learn to windsurf or water ski, or try canoeing or sea kayaking.

Horseback riding is also a great option: ponies for the little ones, and lessons are available for those who have never tried it before, and more challenging rides for children with experience. The overland trails provide great adventure for the whole family to enjoy.

Even a simple walk or bike ride through the woodlands will be entertaining if you let the kids know that it's possible they'll see pigs and piglets in search of chestnuts and other tasty morsels. Corsica is one big nature trail for children whatever season you bring them.

Boat trips can be diverting, as can the *petits trains*, which ride through Ajaccio, Bonifacio, Ille Rouse, Calvi, and Bastia.

The Aqua Cyrné Gliss water park, south of Ajaccio, has slides and plunge pools — for an entirely different kind of fun in the sun and water. The aquarium at l'Île Rousse is small but interesting. A Capulatta, just north of Ajaccio, is a tortoise sanctuary and home to over 2,000 of the creatures, from tiny babies to huge 1 m- (3 ft-) long "monsters" well over 100 years old!

Calendar of Events

Each year, all towns and villages on Corsica celebrate the feast day of their patron saint with a religious procession followed by a carnival or community party. There are too many to list in this guide; contact the Corsican Tourist Authority for details. Listed below are the major events that take place throughout the year.

Spring/variable. *Shrove Tuesday*: island-wide Carnival or Mardi Gras celebrations. *Holy week*: Canistalli procession in Calvi. On Good Friday the Catenacciu takes place at Sartène with other processions in Bonifacio, Calvi, Cargèse, Corte, and Erbalunga. Merendella agricultural fair in the Castagniccia region.

March. Festival of Notre Dame de la Miséricorde in Ajaccio on the 18th.

June. *Early June*: Wine Fair at Luri. *Second Saturday in June*: Historical re-enactment of the arrival of the Genoese Governor in Bastia. *Mid-June*: Festivoce; singing festival at Pigna. *24 June*: Festival of St. Jean Baptiste in Bastia. *Last week in June*: International Jazz festival in Calvi.

August. *First weekend in August*: Napoléon's birthday celebrated in Ajaccio. *Midsummer night*: Fireworks in numerous villages. *Mid-August*: Nonza village in Cap Corse holds a festival of illumination.

September. Les Rencontres Polyphoniques, international a-capella singing contest in Calvi. Also a music festival in the Castagniccia region. *8 September*: Festival of Santa at Casamaccioli. *Last week in September*: Rally in Corsica; five days of cars driving as fast as they can through the countryside, with the start and finish at Ajaccio.

November. The Mediterranean Film Festival in Bastia at the end of the month.

EATING OUT

Corsica's climate and history has had a great effect on their cuisine. Those expecting that this French island will have the same *haute cuisine* as the bistros of Paris are going to be surprised, but not disappointed, by how different the local menu actually is.

The island has always been agricultural, with a wide range of fresh ingredients. The self-sufficient Corsicans have relied on local produce for their traditional dishes; their seasonal menus are generally rustic, filling, and delicious. The macchia supplies wild herbs (rosemary, thyme, marjoram, basil, and fennel) for flavor, and foods preserved for the winter are still made in the traditional manner.

> **Enjoy your meal – *Bon appétit!***

When to Eat

The French have a set meal schedule and Corsica is no exception. Few restaurants stay open throughout the day, even in the large resorts. Breakfast, or *le petit déjeuner*, is available between 7:30–10:30am; coffee and tea, bread and jam, croissants, or *pain au chocolat* (croissant pastry with a chocolate filling) will be available at your hotel at extra cost. In large towns the local café will also have a breakfast menu, which gives you a fine chance to spend some time with the locals. Lunch (*le déjeuner*) takes place between the hours of noon and 2:30pm, dinner (*dîner*) from 6pm. In the high season restaurants stay open late into the evening, usually 11pm or later, though out of season they may close earlier.

Most restaurants offer a *table d'hôte* or set menu for lunch or dinner. These are often four or five courses and represent a good value for the money. *À la carte* (from the menu) dining is also universally available. Lunch is an important social rit-

ual in France and you will find most French people make it the major meal of the day.

If you arrive very early (before Easter) or late (after the end of September) in the season you may find the range of places to eat is limited, as most restaurants are seasonal.

Where to Eat

Seafood restaurants are mostly found along the coast, with meat and game predominating in the countryside. In smaller towns and villages the local hotel usually has a good restaurant. Alternatively, seek out one of the numerous *fermes auberges*; these farms sell their own produce and also serve rustic menus from their own small restaurant during the season. At least 50% of the meal must be produced on the farm. They generally serve meat, charcuterie, and cheeses produced on their own or nearby farms and offer true Corsican cuisine. Menus can be quite basic, but they offer the opportunity to experience a bit more of the island lifestyle.

Corsican soup, accompanied by bread and goat's cheese, is a staple in the local diet.

What to Eat

Corsican charcuterie. The production of *charcuterie* (preserved meats) is an art form throughout France, and on Corsica in particular; the indigenous pigs roam semi-wild or completely wild (*sanglier*), eating a diet of chest-nuts or macchia, each of which gives a particular flavor to the meat. Dried and smoked ham — try *coppa* or *lonza* — are delicious. The meats are smoked with fragrant herbs and wood, and often marinated in wine,

> **Address the waiter as *monsieur*, never as *garçon*. The correct term for a female waiter is *madame* or *mademoiselle*.**

wild rosemary, and garlic to add extra flavor. Paté is also made with these local flavors, but using the liver of the pig.

Appetizers. A hearty soup will often be the start of a Corsican meal. *Suppa corsa*, Corsican soup, has no set recipe but is thick with onions, potatoes, stock, herbs, possi-bly a little pasta, and varying quantities of whichever veg-etables are in season. It is always delicious and makes a fill-ing lunch in itself. *Aziminu* is a type of bouillabaisse using a selection of small fish caught in local waters.

In season you will find snails served in a variety of deli-cious sauces — including mint (*escargots à la menthe*) or anchovy (*escargots aux anchois*). Dried and smoked ham (see charcuterie above), served thinly sliced, is delicious. Most appetizers will be served with a generous helping of Corsican/French bread — freshly baked and crusty. The tra-ditional Corsican accompaniment of chestnut cake or *pulen-ta* is unfortunately now becoming rare.

Meat. Flocks of sheep and goats roam the countryside; you will find roast meats on most menus. Because the meat is so well flavored a simple pork chop (*côte de porc*) or lamb chop (*côte d'agneau*) is a feast in itself. Goat meat is also popu-lar — *mesgisca* is a goat filet.

Most restaurants on Corsica use wood as fuel, producing a char-grilled effect, which is best when done over myrtle with sprigs of a fragrant bush such as juniper. Look out for succulent *cabri* (roast kid), which is an island specialty, or try *raffia*, a skewer of roasted lamb offal.

The slow cooking of meat is another technique used for generations; stews of meat and seasonal vegetables may be found as *cassoulet* on menus. *Tianu di fave* is a kind of pork stew with haricot beans. *Piverunata* is lamb stew with bell peppers.

> **In France an *entrée* is the first course or appetizer; the main course is *le plat principal*.**

In season you will also find rabbit and hare, woodcock, pigeon, and partridge available.

Seafood. Not surprisingly, given its long coastline, seafood (*fruits de mer*) plays an important part in island cuisine. It is not the cheapest option when eating out, however, as catches here, as elsewhere in the Mediterranean, are diminishing, forcing prices to rise. *Assiette de fruits de mer* (literally translated as plate of fruits of the sea), an assortment of fresh seafood which all arrives together, may include mussels (*moules*), spiny lobster (*langoustes*), oysters (*huîtres*), crabs (*crabes*), whelks (*boulots*), shrimps (*crevettes*), and sea urchins (*oursins*). Or try a filet or whole fish, delicately cooked to preserve its freshness. Recommended are sole (*sole*), bream (*dorade*), mullet (*rouget*), or sea bass (*loup de mer*).

The freshwater rivers also produce a delicious trout (*truite*), found on menus inland.

Vegetables. Older people living in the highland villages will have a smallholding and grow their own vegetables, never needing to visit a supermarket. Most fine restaurants will buy from the grower rather than from the wholesale market to ensure freshness. Vegetables are seasonal, which means that you get them at the peak of their flavor, but also that every restaurant is serving the same accompaniment at the same time.

Pizza. Don't be surprised to find pizzas everywhere — they have been cooked in wood-burning stoves here for generations. They come with a variety of toppings and a thin crispy crust.

Cheese. Cheese is as important to the Corsican cuisine as it is in mainland France. The island offers farm produced native cheeses made from sheep and goat milk. *Brocciu* (pronounced briotch) cheese is perhaps the most common. It is a soft-curd cheese traditionally made by farmers in the hillside *bergeries*, or shepherd's huts, which the shepherds could then eat while out in the hills. Now you can taste it, flavored with herbs from the macchia, after your entrée. Brocciu is also used in other dishes such as *fiadone*, a cheesecake flavored with lemon and a little liqueur, or *fritelles de brocciu*, doughnuts of cheese and chestnut flour, deep-fried.

For those who like stronger cheese there is no need to worry — Corsica produces a full range, from mild to pungent, made of cow, sheep, or goat milk.

You will always be offered a seasonal cheese board as well as a dessert menu at the end of your meal.

Dessert. Chestnut (*châtaigne*) flour is the base of a range of pastries and puddings, including *canistrelli*, a sort of

This selection of olives on sale at the Marché Mairie is bound to meet your taste.

bread dough flavored with aniseed (*anis*) or *eau-de-vie* (a distilled liquor literally named "water of life"), which is deep-fried once it has risen. Chestnut flour is also used in Corsican *crêpes*, which are served with a selection of sweet sauces.

Fruit is also seasonal: summer means melons and figs, among other things. Honey is widely available, flavored with the herbs of the macchia and others, including mint (*menthe*) and lavender (*lavande*). The range of flavors is well worth exploring if you are a honey aficionado.

There will be a range of pastries (*pâtisserie*) or cakes (*gâteaux*) on offer at the end of your meal as well as fruit-flavored ice creams (*glaces*) or sorbets.

Drinks. A wide range of drinks are imported from France, including Pastis and Ricard, which are flavored with

Corsican wines are not as renowned as the French, but they have improved enough to merit a sample or two.

aniseed and diluted to taste with cold water. These can be had at all times of day but make a particularly good apéritif. The *Cap Corse* apéritif, produced only on Corsica, is a vermouth-type drink taken over ice. Eau-de-vie is a distilled liquor — perhaps the most famous example is cognac, produced in France. On Corsica eau-de-vie is made from chestnuts, fruit such as mandarin or pear, and *cédrat*, a type of citrus. Pietra is a chestnut beer brewed on the island, while Colomba is a cloudy beer flavored with macchia herbs, which impart a slightly sweet honey flavor. The many tasty beers brewed in northern France and in Italy are also readily available.

Corsica follows the French tradition of drinking bottled water. Local brands are Aqua Corsa, St-Georges, and Zilia. The well-known French and Italian brands are available but are slightly more expensive.

Although you will find fine French wines at better restaurants, it is well worth exploring Corsican varieties. They are rustic in nature, and served cool (*frais*) they complement the local cuisine. Corsican vines suffered a disastrous bout of phyloxerra (a disease that affects vines) in the 19th century, ruining the crop. Because of this, until recently they did not have a good reputation, but standards have improved to such an extent since the 1960s that several have now been awarded *AOC* (*Appellation d'Origine Contrôlée*) status — the standard mark of quality for French wines. These wines will be labeled *Vin de Corse*.

Vin du Pays or country wine, sold by the bottle or the carafe (*pichet*), may be found under *vin de la maison* or house wine on menus. Although it may not have the mark this does not make it a bad wine; it has simply been produced for local consumption, perhaps from a blend of local grapes.

To Help You Order...

Do you have a table for...?	**Avez-vous une table pour...?**
two/three/four people	**deux/trois/quatre personnes**
Do you have a non-smoking table?	**Avez-vous une table non-fumeur?**
Could I have the check?	**L'addition s'il vous plaît.**
Please	**S'il vous plaît**
Thank you	**Merci**
Excuse me	**Excusez-moi/pardon**
I would like (a/an/some)...	**Je voudrais...**

beer	**une bière**	bread	**du pain**
butter	**du beurre**	cheese	**du fromage**
coffee	**un café**	orange juice	**jus d'orange**
tea	**du thé**		

water (sparkling/still)	**de l'eau (gazeuse/non-gazeuse)**
glass/bottle of wine (red/white)	**un verre/une bouteille de vin (rouge/blanc)**

How Would You Like Your Steak?

rare	**saignant**	medium rare	**rose**
medium	**à point**	well done	**bien cuit**

...And Read the Menu

apple	**pomme**	beef	**boeuf**
boar	**sanglier**	chicken	**poulet**
duck	**canard**	garlic	**ail**
green beans	**haricots verts**	ham	**jambon**
lamb	**agneau**	mushroom	**champignon**
onion	**oignon**	pear	**poire**
pepper	**poivre**	pork	**porc**
potatoes	**pommes de terre**	salt	**sel**
		strawberries	**fraises**

HANDY TRAVEL TIPS

An A–Z Summary of Practical Information

Corsica

Note: When calling any French telephone number from outside France, the initial 0 in the number is dropped: dial 00 33 4 and then the eight remaining numbers.

ACCOMMODATION

Hotels. There are around 400 hotels on the island. Any business offering accommodation for visitors without the right of abode (the right to live in Corsica) is graded from 4 stars, Luxe, down to a rating called H.T. — meaning that the establishment conforms to the minimum standards. One-star hotels are said to have average standards. Many hotels are open seasonally, which usually means May–October, and prices rise steeply at peak season (July and August) — often tripling. Always confirm rates for the actual dates you will be traveling before booking. Breakfast is offered at an extra charge, usually between 35 and 40F per person.

All rooms are clean but can be small. Bathrooms are generally smaller than average international rooms, featuring either a shower cubicle or a bath/shower in which you sit rather than stand. Bidets are installed in many bathrooms. Plumbing can be noisy.

Corsica also has *résidence de vacances* and *apart-hotels*, which offer some hotel-style accommodation combined with self-catering amenities — this can mean kitchenettes or full kitchens. Concierge and other hotel services are not standard provision. Vacation villages (*villages de vacances*) offer an inclusive rate with all meals.

The Agence du Tourisme de la Corse issues a booklet with ratings and contact details for all hotels, apart-hotels, and vacation villages.

Self-catering. There are 115 self-catering vacation villages with varying facilities, from a pool and restaurant to a full range of planned sporting activities. It is also possible to rent a cottage or farmhouse — called a *gîtes* — for periods ranging from a few days to a few months. Contact Relais Interdépartemental des Gîtes

Ruraux, 1, rue Général Fiorella – B.P. 10, 20181 Ajaccio, Cedex 1, La Corse; Tel. 04 95 51 72 82; fax 04 95 51 72 89.

Bed & Breakfast. There are an increasing number of families offering B&B accommodation, though this is still not as popular as on mainland France. Look for signs along the road indicating *chambre d'hôte*. Prices may not be cheaper than hotel rooms.

AIRPORT

There are four airports on Corsica, each serving an area roughly equivalent to the sections in this guide. The busiest are Ajaccio and Bastia, but all handle domestic traffic, with flights from Paris and other cities in France.

Below are their names and contact telephone numbers. Figari has the longest transfers from the airport to a major town; it is about 15 minutes from Bonifacio and 20 minutes from Porto-Vecchio. Taxis operate from airport arrival lounges.

Ajaccio: Aéroport Campo Dell'Oro; Tel. 04 95 23 56 56. Bus service from the airport. Taxi fare 100F.

Figari: Aéroport Sud Corse; Tel. 04 95 71 10 10. Taxi transfer only. Airport to Bonifacio 200F.

Bastia: Aéroport de Poretta; Tel. 04 95 54 54 54. Bus service to the airport. Taxi fare 200F.

Calvi: Aéroport de Sainte Catherine; Tel. 04 95 65 88 88. Taxi transfer only. Airport to Calvi 75F.

A few international flights are scheduled to Corsica. The flowing airlines have connections via a European hub: Air France from Paris and Strasbourg to Ajaccio, Bastia, and Calvi; Sabena from Brussels to Ajaccio.

B

BICYCLE RENTAL (*location de bicyclettes*)

Renting a bike for touring the towns or taking to the hills is very simple, but cross-country routes do require a certain level of stamina because of the steep inclines. Always wear protective headgear when cycling and carry fluids in summer to avoid dehydration.

The following companies should be able to help with bikes and other equipment.

Ajaccio: Rout'Evasion, 10 Avenue Noël Franchini; Tel. 04 95 22 72 87

Bastia: Objectif Nature, 3, Rue Notre Dame de Loretta; Tel. 04 95 32 54 34

Bonifacio: Tam Tam Windshop, Route de Santa Manza; Tel. 04 95 73 11 59

Calvi: Garage Ambrosini, Place Christoph Colomb; Tel. 04 95 65 02 13

BUDGETING FOR YOUR TRIP

In general prices are the same on Corsica as in the provinces of France. This means slightly cheaper than in Britain, more expensive than the US, Canada, Australia, and New Zealand. Below is a list of average prices to help clarify your budgeting needs.

Airport transfer by taxi 75–200F.

Day tours per person from 300F.

Hotel room in a moderate establishment mid-season 500F.

Ferry crossing from Nice to Calvi (fast boat), car plus two passengers from 1100F.

Meals. Breakfast at your hotel per person 40F; lunch on set menu (3 courses) without wine at a moderate restaurant per person 90F; dinner on set menu (3 courses) without wine at a moderate restaurant per person 150F; bottle of AOC Corsican wine 90F, *pichet* of *vin maison* 60F.

Museum entrance per adult 35F.

Petit train **ride** around town 35F.

Sports. Speedboat rental for one hour 300F; water-skiing for 15 minutes 150F; kayaking per session 100F; canyoning per day including transport to the site 300F.

Trip to Scandola Reserve from Porto per adult 120F.

Vehicle rental. Weekly rental for a small vehicle 2100F.

CAMPING

Camping is well organized on Corsica and there are nearly 200 campsites to choose from, most with places for tents and caravans, some with places for motor homes. This is a very a popular way of traveling and seeing the islands, so reservations are recommended in the summer months.

The Corsica Tourism Agency has a booklet listing all campsites, the type of camping they can accept, their facilities, and their comfort levels — four stars for very comfortable down to A.N.C (*air naturelle de camping*), which means few facilities in a rural or wild area.

CAR RENTAL/HIRE (*location de voitures*)

Car rental is easy on Corsica, and if you want to explore off the beaten track (much of the interior) it really is the best way to get around. The mountain roads are tortuous — narrow and twisting — but the rewards are well worth the effort.

To rent a car you will need to show your license (which must have been valid for more than one year) and your passport. Many firms have a minimum rental age of 21 and a maximum age of 65 (this varies, so shop around). You will be expected to leave a deposit before you take your car (between 2,000 and 3,000F), though this can be taken from a credit card.

Third-party coverage is compulsory in France; however, it is advisable to take out comprehensive coverage and a collision damage waiver (CDW). Before you do, check with your credit card or domestic insurance company to see if you would already be covered in Corsica. Because of the nature of Corsica's highways, your standard insurance package will not cover damage to parts of the car, such as the suspension, or cover you if you choose to drive off-road.

Below are the contact details for the major companies on the island.

Avis: Ajaccio Airport; Tel. 04 95 23 56 90. Figari Airport; Tel. 04 95 71 00 01. Bastia Airport; Tel. 04 95 36 03 56. Calvi Airport; Tel. 04 95 65 88 38.

Europcar: Ajaccio Airport; Tel. 04 95 23 57 01. Figari Balesi Franchise Porto-Vecchio; Tel. 04 95 73 10 99. Bastia Airport; Tel. 04 95 30 09 50. Calvi; Tel. 04 95 65 10 35.

Hertz: Ajaccio Airport; Tel. 04 95 23 57 04. Figari Gazano Agents; Tel. 04 95 73 00 29. Bastia Airport; Tel. 04 95 30 05 00. Calvi Airport; Tel. 04 95 65 02 96.

Budget: Ajaccio Airport; Tel. 04 95 23 57 21. Bastia Airport; Tel. 04 95 30 05 04. Calvi Airport; Tel. 04 95 65 36 67.

I'd like to rent a car	**Je voudrais louer une voiture**
now/tomorrow	**tout de suite/demain**
for one day/one week	**pour une journée/une semaine**

Moped rental. Although not good for long-distance touring, small mopeds can be useful for visiting the coastal areas and local attractions around each town. They require care on dusty roads or in wet conditions. Always wear a helmet. Contact the following companies:

Ajaccio: Moto Location 51, Cours Napoléon; Tel. 04 95 51 34 45

Bonifacio: Tam-Tam Windshop, Route Santa Manza. Tel. 04 95 73 11 59

Calvi: Ambrosini, 4 Quart Neuf; Tel. 04 95 65 02 13

CLIMATE

Corsica has a complicated climate because of its topography; the temperature at sea level may be vastly different than that in the mountains of the interior.

Winters can be cold, with enough snow in the mountains to support a small skiing industry between January and April. Spring is warm, but can be wet. In summer — May to the end of September — temperatures rise to the high 20s C (low 80s F) with sunny skies, but in the mountains the air can be much cooler and clouds can develop quickly. Fall days can be long and warm.

Generally there is more rain in the north than in the south. The average temperatures are as follows:

	J	F	M	A	M	J	J	A	S	O	N	D
°C	13	13	15	18	21	25	27	28	25	22	17	14
°F	56	57	60	64	69	76	81	82	78	71	63	58

CLOTHING

In summer, light clothing is perfect for the coastal resorts. Beachwear should be worn only on the beach; pack a cover-up to put on during lunch at beachside cafés or in your hotel. Cotton clothing — shorts, slacks, and skirts with shirts or a T-shirt — is ideal for exploring towns in summer. If you plan to visit any churches, women should cover shoulders before they enter and men should not wear shorts. Always carry a light extra layer at night to protect against the cooler breezes.

A good pair of sunglasses is required at all times of year.

If you will be traveling into the mountain regions to walk the trails of the national park or explore the villages, take a layer of warm clothing even in summer; the air can be much cooler than at sea level.

In spring and fall it is always wise to pack a warm layer, a sweater or sweatshirt being ideal.

Corsica

Don't forget to pack stout, comfortable shoes for exploring ancient sites, citadels, and hill villages — many of which have narrow, cobbled streets that can rise at a steep incline.

COMPLAINTS

Complaints should first be taken up with the establishment concerned. If you do not get satisfaction in this manner, approach the local regional administration office; either the *préfecture* in a large town or *sous-préfecture* in a small town. They should be able to assist you further.

CRIME AND SAFETY

Over 50% of all serious crime in France takes place in Corsica, which sounds worrisome. However, these statistics are misleading; the majority of this is violence related to the struggle for liberation directed at the infrastructure of the island (damage done to civic buildings, for instance), or is manifested in domestic, internal feuds — an unauthorized continuation of the vendetta system. Visitors are rarely affected by this or other serious crime and, in fact, could visit the island without realizing that the political struggles were taking place at all.

As with many destinations, petty crimes such as theft do occur, and visitors should take sensible precautions to minimize their risk of becoming victims. Do not flaunt expensive items or large amounts of cash. Leave anything of value in the hotel safe. Do not leave items in rental cars; they are easy for thieves to identify. If you have to, put articles in the trunk of your car, out of sight. Do not leave items unattended on the beach if you go swimming. Always use well-lit streets if you walk late at night.

CUSTOMS (*douane*) AND ENTRY REQUIREMENTS

Most international visitors will have cleared immigration and customs on entry into France, though there are immigration facilities at the main airports on Corsica.

Visas. UK and Irish nationals (and other EU residents) need only some form of identification to enter France. Visitors of US, New Zealand, and Canadian nationality need a valid passport. Australian and South African nationals will need a tourist visa, which can be obtained from the French Embassy in your own country before you depart.

Currency restrictions. There are no restrictions on the amount of French francs or foreign currency that can be imported. You can export unlimited amounts of foreign currency, but you must inform French customs if you wish to export more than 50,000 French francs.

Customs limitations. Travelers from outside Europe may bring in the following duty free goods: 200 cigarettes or 100 cigarillos or 50 cigars or 125 grams of smoking tobacco; 1 liter of spirits or two liters of fortified/sparkling wine; 2 liters of still wine; 50 grams of perfume; 0.25 liters of toilet water.

 D

DRIVING

Driving on Corsica requires a degree of concentration. Corsicans drive far too fast in all conditions, which can be especially disconcerting when you are traversing a mountain pass and meet a Corsican driver coming toward you. If they are behind you and become impatient, allow them to pass by finding the nearest safe place to pull in.

Encounters with pigs, sheep, and cattle are common, so take extra care on blind bends.

Many road signs have been obliterated by hunters' shotgun blasts or painted political slogans. This doesn't mean you are in any danger but can make navigation a challenge. Take a good road map with you to use on any car trip on Corsica.

driver's license	**permis de conduire**
car registration papers	**carte grise**

Corsica

Road conditions. Road conditions are generally good with wide, two-lane highways (single track roads) linking the main towns, and some four-lane highways (dual carriageways) around Ajaccio and Bastia — these are *Route Nationale* or RN roads. *Départmentale* or D roads, linking smaller towns, are generally in good condition. Rural highways or *chemin*, C roads, are the narrowest. Some have undulating surfaces with potholes. There are no toll roads on Corsica.

Though the surfaces are generally good, many mountain roads are narrow and twisting with no shoulders. Always be aware of your position on the road, as many local people drive in the center, rather than on the right, until they see traffic coming in the opposite direction.

Rules and regulations. The French drive on the right, passing on the left. France still operates a *priorité à droite*, or priority from the right, rule, especially in towns — this means that right-of-way is given to vehicles entering the road on your right. This rule is changing in cities and provincial towns, but signs are not always clear, so take extra care. When two roads cross without a junction, there should be a yellow triangle indicating which road has the right of way. This rule does not apply to traffic circles (roundabouts), where priority is given to vehicles already in the circle, i.e. on the left.

Speed limits are 110 km/h (70 mph) on dual highways, on other roads 90 km/h (55 mph), in town 50 km/h (30 mph). All limits are reduced in wet weather and in foggy conditions.

Seat belts are compulsory, as are crash helmets for motorbikes and mopeds.

France operates an "on the spot" fine system; if you commit an offense you will be required to pay the officer who stops you. Drunk-driving rules are strict, with on-the-spot fines — and re-possession of the vehicle in serious cases. Random breath tests are undertaken at roadsides, and your vehicle could be impounded by police.

Fuel costs. Fuel (*essence*) is expensive in France, at 8F per liter. Many cars run on diesel fuel (*gazole*), which is much cheaper. Keep your gas tank as full as possible — fill up in major towns as you pass to ensure that you don't run out — because in country areas fuel stops are few. Some fuel stations have pumps that operate 24 hours per day if you pay by credit card, though these are found only in major towns.

Fluid measures

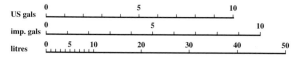

Parking. Parking is difficult in the major towns. Street parking is acceptable except where there are yellow curbs, or where an official sign indicates restrictions. Several parking lots (indicated by a blue sign with the white letter P) have been created; some are free but others charge on entrance, so have some small change available.

If you need help. If you are traveling with your own vehicle, buy international breakdown coverage for the length of your journey before you leave home. This will help you get aid in case of an emergency and will cover the cost of most repairs. In the UK contact the Automobile Association; Tel. 0800 444500 (toll-free in UK), or the RAC; Tel. 0870 572 2722. In the US contact AAA; Tel. (800) 222-4357 (toll-free in US).

Your car rental company should be able to supply the contact details of a reliable recovery company in case you have problems. Always examine your vehicle carefully before setting out, especially if you plan to drive in remote parts of the island.

Taking your own car to Corsica. You must carry your car registration, proof of insurance, valid driver's license, and red warning triangle to put on the road if you break down or have an accident. Your car must display a national ID sticker. Your headlights must be adjusted or deflected for right hand driving. If you are bringing your car from the UK, purchase a Green Card, which offers full insurance coverage when abroad. If you already have comprehensive insurance you may be able to arrange this extra coverage free of charge.

Road signs. France uses the international symbols for road signs, but here are a few others you may find on your journey.

déviation	diversion/detour
péage	toll
priorité à droite	yield to traffic from the right
vous n'avez pas la priorité	give way
ralentir	slow down
serrez à droite/à gauche	keep right/left
sens unique	one way
rappel	restriction continues (a reminder)

E

ELECTRICITY

France operates on 22 volts with two- or three-pronged, round-pinned plugs. You will need to buy an adapter to use your electrical appliances. US appliances will also need a transformer.

EMBASSIES AND CONSULATES

All major embassies and consulates are situated in Paris. Contact information is as follows.

Australia: (embassy) 4, rue Jean Rey, 75724 Paris; Tel. (33) 01 40 59 33 00; fax (33) 01 40 59 33 10; web site <www.austgov.fr>

Canada: (embassy) 35, avenue Montaigne, 75008 Paris; Tel. (33) 01 44 43 29 00; fax (33) 01 44 43 29 99; web site <www. amb-canada.fr>

New Zealand: (embassy) 7th Floor, rue Léonardo de Vinci, 75116 Paris; Tel. (33) 01 45 10 43 43; fax (33) 01 45 01 43 44

Republic of Ireland: (embassy) 4, rue Rude, 75016 Paris; Tel. (33) 01 45 00 20 87; fax (33) 01 45 00 84 17

South Africa: (embassy) 59, quai d'Orsay, 75007 Paris; Tel. (33) 01 53 59 23 23

UK: (embassy) 35, rue du Fauborg Saint-Honoré, 75008 Paris; Tel. (33) 01 42 66 91 42; fax (33) 01 44 51 34 83; web site <www. amb-grandbretagne.fr>

US: (embassy) 2, avenue Gabriel, 75008 Paris; Tel. (33) 01 43 12 22 22; fax. (33) 01 42 66 97 83

EMERGENCIES

In case of fire, call the fire service (*sapeurs pompiers*); Tel. 18. They can also provide first aid and ambulance service. If you need an ambulance (*samu*); Tel. 15. Police (*gendarmes*); Tel. 17.

Local numbers for police in a non-emergency situation are: Ajaccio, 04 95 29 21 47; Bastia, 04 95 54 50 22; Calvi, 04 95 65 00 17; Porto Vecchio, 04 95 70 00 17.

G

GETTING THERE

By Air

Scheduled flights connect with Corsica from Paris and Strasbourg with Air France; web site <www.airfrance.com> and Bruxelles/Brussels with Sabena; web site <www.sabena.com>. There are numerous connections from the US, Australia, New Zealand, and South Africa to these two destinations for continuing flights.

British Airways operates services with transfer at Nice or Marseilles; web site <www.britishairways.com>

Corsica

Numerous charter companies operate flights from French airports to Corsica. Contact Air Liberté; Tel. 04 95 71 10 10.

Simply Corsica is a UK company that specializes in self-catering villa and apartment holidays to Corsica; Tel. 020 8541 2205; web site <www.simply-travel.com>.

By Sea

There are several routes from the coasts of France and Italy to the six major ports on Corsica: Bastia, Ajaccio, Calvi, Porto-Vecchio, l'Île-Rousse, and Bonifacio. The major ports on the southern French coast are Marseilles, Nice, and Toulon. Fast boats (*navires rapides*) carry passengers from Nice to Calvi in 2¹/2 hours — the fastest crossing — but these do not run in bad weather. Normal ferryboats take over twice as long (Nice to Ajaccio in 7 hours) but are more reliable and run throughout the year. Always make a reservation for your crossing if you are traveling in high season. Contact the following companies:

S.N.C.M/Ferryterranee sails from the French ports of Marseilles, Nice, and Toulon, offering both ferryboats and *navires rapides* services; Tel. 08 36 67 95 00 in France, 0207 491 4968 in the UK.

Corsica Ferries sails from Nice, Livourne, and Savone; Tel. 04 95 32 95 95.

Corsica Marittima sails from Genes (Genoa) and Livourne. Contact S.N.C.M for details.

Car travel to the ferry ports. From the UK, vehicles must first get to the European mainland. Most popular routes are ferry crossings from Calais to Dover with companies such as Sea France; Tel. 08705 711 711; web site <www.seafrance.com>, or through the channel tunnel; Tel. 0800 096 9992 (toll-free in UK); web site <www.eurotunnel.com>.

Once in France, the comprehensive motorway network (*autoroute*) will allow you to travel at speed to the ports. The main routes are the A7 via Dijon and Lyon or the A62 via Bordeaux and Toulouse. These are toll roads, and cost approximately 300F. Main RN routes are free but will add time to the journey.

Coach travel to ferry ports. Eurolines operates bus/coach services that connect many cities in Europe, including Paris, Brussels, and London with Nice and Marseilles, for onward connection to Corsica. Contact them at <www.eurolines.com>, or, in the UK; Tel. 0990 143291. Their main office in Paris is at 22, Rue Malmaison, 93177 Bagnolet; Tel. 01 49 72 57 80; fax 01 49 72 57 99.

Rail travel to the ferry ports. Train services in France, including passenger and vehicle trains, are operated by SNCF (Société Nationale des Chemins de Fer). Information and reservations; Tel. 01 45 82 50 50. Comprehensive information on rail services, including prices throughout Europe, can be found at <www.eurorail.com>.

GUIDES AND TOURS

Walking tours. The tourist offices at Ajaccio, Bastia, Calvi, and Porto Vecchio offer guided tours of the old towns (including museums and monuments) in summer. Cap Corse can also be explored with qualified guides. Contact Cap Corse Association, 4 parc Saint Victor, 20200 Ville de Pietrabugno; Tel. 04 95 32 72 42.

To organize guided walks in the forests contact the Office National des Forêts, Centre Administratif. Nouveau Port, 20407 Bastia; Tel. 04 95 32 81 90; fax 04 95 32 61 63.

Bus tours. Several companies offer coach trips by the day or half-day to main attractions and sites. This is a good way to view the mountainous areas such as the Col de Bavella if you don't want to drive. Contact details are as follows:

Ajaccio: Autocars Ollandini, 1 route d'Alata; Tel. 04 95 23 92 40
Porto-Vecchio: Autocars les Rapides Bleus, 7 rue Juarès; Tel. 04 95 70 10 36

Corsica

Bastia: Autocars Kallisttour, 6 Avenue Maréchal Sebastiani; Tel. 04 95 31 71 49

Calvi: Autocars Mariani/Corse Voyages, Val de Legno RN 197; Tel. 04 95 65 00 47

HEALTH AND MEDICAL CARE

There are no major health risks when visiting Corsica. The majority of problems relate to diarrhea and sunburn. Taking a few simple preventative steps can alleviate both of these ailments.

Limit your time in the sun during your first few days. Wear a hat, apply sun protection products regularly, and always carry a cover-up in case of overexposure. Wear sunglasses to avoid eye-strain.

For stomach problems, avoid too much alcohol. Rest and keep fluid levels high if you do become ill.

Corsica has a modern healthcare network but not all doctors speak English well. There are three major hospitals in south Corsica and four in the north. In addition you will find numerous day clinics, which can deal with minor ailments such as wounds, sprains, or minor sunburn.

Pharmacies also have staff qualified to advise on ailments such as stomach-ache and diarrhea or colds, and they will have a good range of medicines available over the counter.

Two hospitals in the major towns are: Centre Hospitalier Départemental de Castelluccio in Ajaccio; Tel. 04 95 29 36 36, and Centre Hospitalier Général Paese Nouvo in Bastia: Tel. 04 95 77 95 00.

Visitors from Great Britain and Ireland will be treated without charge provided they carry Form E111 fully completed and verified at any post office. Other nationalities will be charged for treatment; for minor aid this may involve paying in cash and reclaiming the money from your insurance company yourself. Always make sure that you are covered by insurance adequate for emergency health problems.

If you wish to enjoy some of the more exhilarating sports (climbing/rafting/para-ponting), do check the small print of your insurance, as you may need to take out extra coverage; do not participate in these sports without being sure of your coverage. If you get lost or hurt on a hiking route or other remote place, recovery can be expensive.

HITCHHIKING

Hitchhiking is not illegal on Corsica, however, be aware that you may find yourself being dropped off at remote sites with no passing traffic. Traveling alone with strangers can obviously be dangerous and is not advised.

HOLIDAYS

The following days are official public holidays in Corsica.

1 January	*Jour de l'An* (New Year's Day)
March or April	*Ascension* (Easter Sunday)
	Lundi de Pâques (Easter Monday)
1 May	*Fête du Travail* (Labor Day)
late May	*Lundi de Pentacôte* (Whit Monday)
14 July	*Fête Nationale* (Bastille Day)
15 August	*Assomption* (Assumption)
1 November	*Toussaint* (All Saints Day)
11 November	*Anniversaire de l'Armistice* (Armistice Day)
25 December	*Noël* (Christmas Day)

L

LANGUAGE

French is the official language of Corsica, though many people also speak Corsi — an amalgamation of old Italian and Latin. Modern Italian is also widely spoken, along with some English.

Corsica

The local people will always appreciate your attempts to speak to them in French, so try to use the language tips throughout this guide. For more comprehensive help, the *Berlitz French Phrase Book and Dictionary* covers almost all situations you're likely to encounter in your travels.

Here are some language pointers to help with your trip to Corsica.

French is pronounced much differently than English. The words are unstressed, which means that each syllable in the word is given equal emphasis.

Numbers

one	**un, une**	six	**six**
two	**deux**	seven	**sept**
three	**trois**	eight	**huit**
four	**quatre**	nine	**neuf**
five	**cinq**	ten	**dix**

Days of the Week

Monday	**lundi**	Friday	**vendredi**
Tuesday	**mardi**	Saturday	**samedi**
Wednesday	**mercredi**	Sunday	**dimanche**
Thursday	**jeudi**		

Do you speak English?	**Parlez-vous anglais?**
I am American/English.	**Je suis américain/anglais.**
How much is it?	**C'est combien?**
My name is…	**Je m'appelle…**
I don't understand.	**Je ne comprends pas.**
Where is…	**Où est…**

…the bank   **…la banque**

…post office   **…la poste**

LAUNDRY AND DRY CLEANING

There are coin-operated laundries at the following pleasure ports: Bastia, Bonifacio, Calvi, Porto-Vecchio, and Macinoggio.

MAPS

Michelin makes a comprehensive map of Corsica. For those planning hiking/walking routes, the Institut Géographique National (IGN) maps offer official routes and terrain details. These are available at stores across the island.

MEDIA

Few hotels offer English-speaking TV stations as part of their service. The main French station, TF1, is always available, along with a range of satellite channels in French and Italian. Most English/US programs are dubbed into French, though on Italian channels they may have subtitles instead of dubbing.

Foreign newspapers are available at most major newsagents in the main coastal resorts, though these may be at least one day old. There is a cyber-café on the harborfront at Calvi for those who want to get on-line.

MONEY

Currency. Corsica uses the French franc as currency. It is signified by the letter F before or after the amount. At international exchange offices and banks FF will be used, to distinguish it from the Belgian or Swiss Franc.

Each Franc is made up of 100 centimes, abbreviated c or ct. Notes (*billets*) are printed in the following denominations: 20F, 50F, 100F, 200F, 500F. Coins (*pièces*) as 5c, 10c, 20c, 50c, 1F, 2F, 5F, 10F, 20F. Most French banks operate a currency exchange facility. These are generally open Monday–Friday 9am–4:30pm (some close for lunch). Always carry your passport when you change money or cash traveler's checks.

Many hotels will offer an exchange service, but the rates will be less favorable than at a bank.

Credit cards (*cartes bancaires*). Credit cards are widely accepted at hotels, restaurants, and shops. They can be used to obtain cash at ATMs and over the counter at banks.

ATMs (*distributeurs automatiques de billets*). The ATM network on Corsica is growing, and you will find international ATM facilities in Ajaccio, Calvi, and Bastia. Contact your ATM provider for up-to-date details before you depart.

Traveler's checks. Traveler's checks are widely accepted both for payment and to obtain cash at banks and hotels. Always carry identification when cashing traveler's checks.

OPEN HOURS

Most settlements in Corsica take a lunch break and afternoon opening hours can be erratic, so if you have any important or official business it is best taken care of in the morning, when you are more likely to find the person you need in the office.

Banks are generally open 9am–4:30pm (some close at lunchtime, especially in small towns).

Main post offices are open from 8am–7pm Monday–Friday, 9am–noon on Saturdays.

Museums are usually open daily 9am–5pm (though they can be open later, especially in summer). Some are closed Monday or Tuesday and all national holidays.

Shops are open from 8am–noon and again from 4pm–7pm. Many close from Saturday lunchtime until Tuesday morning (shops in tourist areas may be open longer hours and remain open on Sundays and Mondays).

 P

POLICE

Uniformed police (blue trousers and black jackets) keep order and direct traffic. They patrol in blue vehicles and also on foot in resort areas. They may not speak English, but will in general be courteous and helpful.

In Calvi you may see military police patrols. They oversee the activities of soldiers based in the area.

POST OFFICES

Post offices have yellow signs with *La Poste* (the post office) in blue letters. Signs to post offices may say P.T.T, which stands for *postes, télégraphes, téléphones*. Mail service is reliable.

When mailing a letter or card you may find two slots. One will have a local box and another with *autres directions* on it. This box is used for long distance and international mail.

Post offices sell stamps, phone cards, and money orders. Stamps and phone cards can also be purchased at *tabacs*, the small tobacconist/news kiosks.

Postcards cost 3F to Europe, 4.5F for farther afield.

PUBLIC TRANSPORTATION

Bus. Bus services run between the major towns but are not an ideal way of seeing the island, as they take a long time between remote settlements. Contact the Gare Routière at Quai Herminier in Ajaccio (next door to the port); Tel. 04 95 51 55 45.

Train. Chemins de Fer de la Corse operates two main services that link Calvi with Ajaccio and Calvi with Bastia. The services cross at Ponte Leccia, enabling transfer between lines. This service is called the Trinighallu and is one of the best ways to see Corsica's landscape. Prices are cheap — around 50F for a single journey. For details contact the stations in the following towns: Ajaccio; Tel. 04 95 23 11 03, Bastia; Tel. 04 95 32 80 61, Calvi; Tel. 04 95 65 00 61. Automatic ticket machines can be found at the stations. These take coins and credit cards, or you can also pay at a ticket counter.

There is also an extra service which operates from Calvi north along the coast to l'Île-Rousse, stopping at many small stations on the route. Called the tramway de Balagne, it links the major tourist resorts with a string of beaches on this coastline. Call for details from Calvi; Tel. 04 95 65 00 61 or l'Île-Rousse; Tel. 04 95 60 00 50.

R

RELIGION
Corsica is predominantly Roman Catholic, with a minority Orthodox community in Cargèse on the west coast. Each community has a yearly festival to celebrate its patron saint's day, and many establishments, including shops, close on Sunday.

T

TELEPHONE
The international code for France is 33.

When calling from outside France, the initial 0 in French telephone numbers is dropped: dial 00 33 4 and then the eight remaining numbers.

Use the following codes when making international calls from France; again, dial 00 before the international country code and omit the initial 0 in the area code.

Australia	61	Canada	1
Ireland	353	New Zealand	64
South Africa	27	UK	44
US	1		

Payphones in France generally take both coins and phone cards. Cards can be purchased at post offices, *tabacs* (tobacconists), and newsstands. Many cafés also have payphones for customer use. Post offices have telephone *cabines* where you can make long distance and international calls, and pay after you have finished. This will be cheaper than calling direct from your hotel. More convenient is to have an international call provider with an access number. AT&T and other companies offer this kind of service and will charge calls to your credit card.

Minitel. France operates a national system, called Minitel, which provides a variety of services on a small screen and keyboard via the telephone lines. Many businesses such as hotels, and transportation providers such as airlines and trains, have a minitel number linking to information or booking services.

TIME ZONES

France operates on Central European Time (CET). This is one hour ahead of Greenwich Mean Time (GMT).

New York	London	**Corsica**	Sydney	Auckland
6am	11am	**noon**	8pm	10pm

France uses the 24-hour clock when posting times. This means that 9am is 09.00 and 9pm is 21.00.

TIPPING

All hotel and restaurant/café bills will have a service charge included in the price. There is no obligation to leave a tip unless you feel tthat the service was exceptional. However, many people continue the practice of leaving small change when they visit bars and cafés.

Taxi drivers	10%
Chambermaids	20F per day
Tour guide	10%
Hotel porter	5F per bag

TOILETS

There are few public toilets around the island. If you use the facilities in a café or bar, you should buy a drink there before you leave. Most tourist attractions have good facilities.

Where is the rest room please? **Où sont les toilettes s'il vous plaît?**

TOURIST INFORMATION

The Corsican Tourist Office can be contacted at the following address: Agence du Tourisme de la Corse, 17 Boulevard Roi-Jérôme, 20181 Ajaccio, France; Tel. 04 95 51 00 00; fax 04 95 51 14 40; web site <www2.sitec.fr/atc>.

If you require information about Corsica before you leave on your trip, contact the French Tourist Office (Les Maisons de la France) in your country.

Australia: French Tourist Bureau, 25 Bligh Street, Level 22, Sydney, NSW 2000; Tel. 292 315255; fax 292 218682; web site <www.franceguide.trav.net>

Canada: Maison de la France, 1981 Mac Gill College, Suite 490 Esso Tower, Montreal Quebec H3A 2W9; Tel. (514) 288 4264; fax (514) 845 4868; web site <www.franceguide.com>

Ireland: Maison de la France, 10 Suffolk Street, Dublin 2; Tel. (1) 679 0813; fax (1) 679 0814

South Africa: Maison de la France, P.O. Box 41022, Craighall 2024; Tel. 11 880 8062; fax 11 770 1666; web site <www.frenchdoor.co.za>

UK: Maison de la France, 178 Piccadilly, London W1V 0AL; Tel. 207 399 3500; fax 207 493 6594; web site <www.franceguide.com>

US: Maison de la France, 444 Madison Avenue, New York, NY 10022; Tel. (212) 838 7800; fax (212) 838 7855; web site <www.francetourism.com>

Maison de la France, 676 North Michigan Avenue, Chicago, Ill 60611; Tel. (312) 751 7800; fax (312) 337 6339; web site <www.francetourism.com>

Maison de la France, 9454 Wilshire Boulevard, Suite 715, Beverly Hills, CA 901212; Tel. (310) 271 6665; fax (310) 276 2835; web site <www.francetourism.com>

There are 31 local tourist offices in towns and villages on Corsica: these may be signposted Office du Tourisme or Syndicats d'Initiative. The addresses of the major offices are as follows:

Bastia: Place Saint Nicholas 20410 Bastia; Tel. 04 95 55 96 96

Bonifacio: La Citadelle, 20169 Bonifacio; Tel. 04 95 73 11 88

Calvi: Port de Plaisance, 20260 Calvi; Tel. 04 95 65 16 67

Corte: Fontaine des Quatre Canons, 20250 Corte; Tel. 04 95 46 26 70

l'Île-Rousse: Place Paoli, 20220 l'Île Rousse; Tel. 04 95 60 04 35

Porto-Vecchio: Cité Administrative, 20144 Sainte-Lucie de Porto-Vecchio; Tel. 04 95 71 48 99

Sartène: 6 Rue Borgo, 20100 Sartène; Tel. 04 95 77 15 40

WEB SITES

Relevant web sites for organizations mentioned in this guide are included along with their other contact details. However, below are several web sites that offer general information about the island and provide links to other helpful sites.

Corsica

<www.internet.com.fr/corsica/uk/venir>

<www.corsicaonline.com>

<www.corsenet.com>

<www.corsica_nazione.com>

<www.concierge.com>

WEIGHTS AND MEASURES

France uses the metric system.

Length

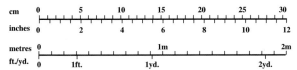

Weight

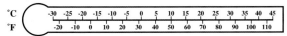

Temperature

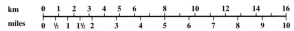

Distance

km and miles scale

Y

YOUTH HOSTELS (*auberges de jeunesse*).

The Fédération Unie des Auberges de Jeunesse (FUEJ), 27 Rue Pajol, 75018 Paris; Tel. 01 44 98 87 27 will supply a free book listing youth hostels throughout France.

Recommended Hotels

There are no large resort hotels on Corsica. Most are between 30 and 40 rooms, over 50 rooms being considered large; many are family-owned and -run. They are usually open only "in season"; generally from Easter through October, but some open as late as the end of May and can close at the end of September. Make sure you confirm annual closing periods (*fermeture annuelle*) before traveling out of season.

Most hotel rates go up and down during the season; the highest rates are charged from the end of July to the end of August, corresponding with French and Italian school vacation. Prices can treble between low and high dates and may vary depending on the location of a room in the hotel. For example, sea views and balconies will have a price premium. Do confirm with the hotel the price for the exact dates and room that you want before making a reservation.

Room prices include a room tax of 4F per night but not breakfast, which will cost around 35–40F per person.

Bathrooms and plumbing have a particular character in many French hotels; shower cubicles are small or bathrooms will have showers with no curtain. (Sit to shower if you don't want the whole room to get wet.) Bidets are common. Soap is usually provided but not shampoo. There may be a TV in the room but there won't be English language channels — French and Italian are most common. Many French hotels accept pets.

The following hotels vary in style but each has a particular attraction, be it location, value, or service. The accompanying price guides indicate prices per room per night at mid to low season.

When calling any French telephone number from outside France, the initial 0 in the number is dropped: dial 00 33 4 and then the eight remaining numbers.

$$$$$	over 800F
$$$$	650–800F
$$$	500–650F
$$	350–500F
$	under 350F

THE SOUTHWEST

Eden Roc Hôtel $$$$ *Route des Sanguinaires, 2000 Ajaccio; Tel. 04 95 51 56 00; fax 04 95 52 05 03*. Situated on the route west from Ajaccio, across from a sandy beach, the Eden Roc offers everything needed for a relaxing vacation. Rooms have A/C, TV, mini-bar. Facilities include restaurant, pool, sauna, Jacuzzi, garden, parking. Open all year. 36 rooms. Major credit cards.

Hôtel Costa $$–$$$ *2 Rue Colomba, 2000 Ajaccio; Tel. 04 95 21 43 03; fax 04 95 21 59 82*. Set in a residential area just a 10-minute stroll along the seafront to the old town, the Hotel Costa makes a good, cost-effective base for touring the southwest. Rooms are large with simple furnishings. TV, phone. Facilities include small garden, guarded parking for an extra fee. Open all year. 53 rooms. Major credit cards.

Le Maquis $$$$$ *B.P. 94, 20166 Porticcio; Tel. 04 95 25 05 55; fax 04 95 25 11 70*. One of the best hotels on the island, with luxurious fittings and attention to detail not always found in other establishments. The hotel has a private beach and all rooms have views over the Gulf of Ajaccio. Rooms have A/C, phone, TV, mini-bar. Facilities include pool, excellent restaurant, pool, tennis, garden, parking. 30 rooms. Handicapped accessible. Open all year. Major credit cards.

Villa Piana $$–$$$ *Route de Propriano, 20100 Sartène; Tel. 04 95 77 07 04; fax 04 95 73 45 65*. Good hotel with magnificent mountain views, looking across to the citadel of Sartène. Pretty restaurant terrace and nice pool. Rooms, on the small side, are thoughtfully decorated. Rooms have phone. Facilities include restaurant, tennis, garden, parking. Handicapped accessible. Open Apr–Oct. 31 rooms. Major credit cards.

THE SOUTHEAST

Grand Hôtel de Cala Rossa $$$$$ *Cala Rossa, 20137 Porto-Vecchio; Tel. 04 95 71 61 51; fax 04 95 71 60 11; web site <www.relaischateaux.fr/calarossa>*. Beautiful white-washed hotel set amid fragrant pine trees 10 km (6 miles) north of Porto Vecchio. A relaxing place to return after a day's touring. Fine restaurant and terrace overlooking the gulf. Prices include evening meal. Closed 1 Nov–1 Apr. 55 rooms. Major credit cards.

Hôtel Genovese $$$–$$$$ *Quartier de la Citadelle, 20169 Bonifacio; Tel. 04 95 73 12 34; fax 04 95 73 09 03*. Interesting hotel (it was once the archbishop's palace but has been totally refurbished) set in the old town; a perfect base for exploring the citadel. Rooms have A/C, phone, TV, mini-bar. Facilities include garden and parking. Closed 1 Nov–1 Mar. 14 rooms. Major credit cards.

Hôtel Roi d'Aragon $$–$$$ *13 Quai Comparetti, 20169 Bonifacio; Tel. 04 95 73 03 99; fax 04 95 73 07 94*. Situated on the portside below the citadel, this hotel is an ideal base for restaurants in the port and boat tours. Rooms at the front overlook the harbor; those on the top floor have balconies. Rooms have A/C, TV, phone. Pay to park in the port. Open all year. 31 rooms. Major credit cards.

Le Belvedere $$$$$ *Route de Palombaggia, 20137 Porto-Vecchio; Tel. 04 95 70 54 13; fax 04 95 70 42 63*. Set above the wonderful bay of Palombaggia and surrounded by vegetation, the Belvedere is a relaxing place to stay. Situated 5 km (2½ miles) south of Porto-Vecchio. There are both bungalows and rooms available. Rooms include A/C, TV, phone, mini-bar. Facilities include pool, tennis, sauna, Jacuzzi, garden, parking. Prices include evening meal. Handicapped accessible. Closed 1 Jan–1 Apr. 19 rooms. Major credit cards.

Le Moby Dick $$$$ *Golfe de Santa Guilia, B.P. 24, 20137 Porto-Vecchio; Tel. 04 95 70 70 00; fax 04 95 70 71 01.* Set by the beautiful beach of Santa Guilia and its Caribbean-like vistas, this hotel is a good base for couples and families. Rooms have A/C, TV, phone, mini-bar. Facilities include 113 rooms and cabins, restaurant, tennis. Handicapped accessible. Closed 1 Oct–1 Apr. Major credit cards.

Sole e Monti $$ *20122 Quenza; Tel. 04 95 78 62 53; fax 04 95 78 63 88.* Well placed for touring the Col de Bavella and surrounding footpaths of the Alta Rocca, this hotel on the main street of the village of Quenza has great ambience. Bathrooms are a little small. Rooms have TV, phone. Facilities include good restaurant serving local cuisine. Closed 1 Oct–1 May. 20 rooms. Major credit cards.

U Benedettu $$$$ *20137 Lecci de Porto-Vecchio; Tel. 04 95 71 62 81; fax 04 95 71 66 37.* Small hotel on a sandy beach just five minutes' drive north of Porto-Vecchio. Accomodations include larger studio and family cabins for longer-term guests. Rooms have A/C, phone, TV, mini-bar. Facilities include garden, parking. Handicapped accessible. 29 rooms. Open all year. Major credit cards.

THE NORTHEAST AND CAP CORSE

Castel Brando $$–$$$ *B.P. 20, 20222 Brando, Erbalunga; Tel. 04 95 30 10 30; fax 04 95 33 98 18.* This 19th-century mansion set in a garden by the sea in the small hamlet of Castel Brando is now a family-run hotel. Rooms have A/C, phone, and TV. Facilities include pool, garden, parking. Handicapped accessible. Closed 1 Oct–21 Apr. 21 rooms. Major credit cards.

Hôtel de la Corniche $$$ *San-Martino-di-Lota, 20200 Bastia; Tel. 04 95 31 40 98; fax 04 95 32 37 69.* Located only 10 minutes by car from Bastia, in a hillside village with wonderful views. This simple hotel is a good value. Rooms have TV, phone. Facilities include a locally renowned restaurant, pool, garden, parking. Closed January. 19 rooms. Major credit cards.

Hôtel le Caribou $$$ *20228 Porticciola; Tel. 04 95 35 02 33; fax. 04 95 35 01 13.* On the far side of the coast road near Porticciola, this hotel is full of character, with stained-glass windows and Moorish tiles. It is set in verdant gardens across from a sandy beach. Rooms have phone. Facilities include restaurant, pool, tennis, sauna, Jacuzzi, parking. Handicapped accessible. Closed 1 Oct–1 July. 44 rooms. Major credit cards.

Hôtel le Refuge $$ *20229 Piedicroce; Tel. 04 95 35 82 65; fax 04 95 35 84 42.* Set in the heart of the Castagniccia region and a good base for exploring by vehicle or on foot, this simple hotel offers a quiet escape from resort activities on the coast. Rooms have phone. Facilities include restaurant serving a daily local menu. Closed 1 Dec–31 Mar. 20 rooms. Major credit cards.

Hôtel Pietracap $$$ *20, route de San-Martino, Pietranera, 20200 Bastia; Tel. 04 95 31 61 85; fax 04 95 31 39 00.* Situated 3 km (1 3 miles) north of Bastia's center in a quiet residential area, this hotel has beautiful gardens and a pool. There is no restaurant on the premises. Good-sized rooms have A/C, TV, phone, safe, mini-bar, parking. Handicapped accessible. Closed 1 Dec–31 Mar. 35 rooms. Major credit cards.

Hôtel Treperi $$$ *20217 Saint-Florent; Tel. 04 95 37 40 20; fax 04 95 37 04 61.* Pretty hotel on the route to Bastia a few minutes from the center of town. Set in a large garden with views over the Gulf of Saint-Florent. Rooms are simply decorated and have TV, phone. Facilities include restaurant, pool, tennis, parking. Closed 1 Oct–1 Mar. 18 rooms. Major credit cards.

Le Vieux Moulin $$ *Le Port, 20238 Centuri; Tel. 04 95 35 60 15; fax 04 95 35 60 24.* Situated above the old port at Centuri, this fine 19th-century mansion with vine-covered walls is a most impressive site. Rooms in the annex have more up-to-date facilities, but the atmosphere of the main house and the restaurant are not to be missed. Rooms have TV, phone. Facilities include tennis, garden, parking. 14 rooms. Major credit cards.

U Sant'Agnellu $–$$ *20247 Rogliano; Tel. 04 95 35 40 59; fax 04 95 35 40 59.* A small rustic hotel in the mountains at the very northern tip of Cap Corse, with basic rooms but breathtaking views over the coastline and surrounding peaks. Facilities include restaurant, garden, parking. Closed 1 Oct–1 Apr. 9 rooms. Major credit cards.

THE NORTHWEST

Auberge de la Signorina $$$$ *Route de la Fôret de Bonifatu, 20260 Calvi; Tel. 04 95 65 93 00; fax 04 95 65 38 77.* Large house surrounded by vegetation converted into a country-style hotel. All services are of a high standard. Rooms have A/C, phone, TV, mini-bar. Facilities include restaurant, pool, tennis, parking. Open 1 Apr–30 Sept. 10 rooms. Major credit cards.

Hôtel Amiral $$ *Boulevard de la Mer, 20220 l'Île-Rousse; Tel. 04 95 60 28 05; fax 04 95 60 31 21.* Situated across the street from the sandy beach, this modern hotel offers simple accommodation and is well positioned for touring the region or just relaxing. Five minutes' walk to the center of town. Rooms have A/C, phone. Parking for hotel guests. Closed 1 Oct–31 Mar. 20 rooms. Major credit cards.

Hôtel Cappo Rosso $$$–$$$$ *Route des Calanches, 20115 Piana; Tel. 04 95 27 82 40; fax 04 95 27 80 00.* Set above the rugged calanche rocks, this hotel offers a peaceful getaway with 4-star standards. Rooms have TV, phone, mini-bar. Facilities include fine restaurant with panoramic views, pool, garden, parking. Handicapped accessible. Closed 1 Oct–31 Mar. 57 rooms. Major credit cards.

Hôtel Mare et Monti $$ *20225 Feliceto; Tel. 04 95 63 02 00; fax 04 95 63 02 01.* Family owned since 1870, this hotel sits by the river in a tiny mountain village. Rooms have phone. Facilities include garden, parking. Closed 1 Oct–1 Apr. 18 rooms. Major credit cards.

Corsica

La Villa $$$$$ *Chemin de Notre-Dame-de-la-Serra, 20260 Calvi; Tel. 04 95 65 10 10; fax 04 95 65 10 10; web site <www.relaischateaux.fr/lavilla>.* Beautiful views across Calvi Bay from the terrace of this hotel, which is set on a hillside 7 km (4.3 miles) from town. One of the finest hotels on the island. Rooms have A/C, phone, TV, mini-bar. Facilities include restaurant, 3 pools, tennis, sauna/Jacuzzi, activities, parking. Closed 2 Jan–31 Mar. Handicapped accessible. 34 rooms. Major credit cards.

Les Roches Rouge $–$$ *20115 Piana; Tel. 04 95 27 81 81; fax 04 95 27 81 76.* Located in an imposing 19th-century building, this hotel has a look of faded grandeur about it. The rooms are simple and rustic, with good views across the countryside and eastern access to the calanche area. Rooms have phone. Facilities include parking, garden. Open 1 Apr–31 Oct. 30 rooms. Major credit cards.

Napoléon Bonaparte $$$–$$$$ *Place Paoli, 20220 I'Île-Rousse; Tel. 04 95 60 06 09; fax 04 95 60 11 51.* This hotel is the oldest in the region, set in a beautiful building on the main square. If you'd like to enjoy the grandeur of a bygone French age, then this is the place for you. The delights of I'Île-Rousse lie just a few minutes' stroll away. Rooms have phone. Facilities include pool, tennis, garden, parking. Closed 1 Oct–31 Mar. 90 rooms. Major credit cards.

The Balanea $$$–$$$$ *6, Rue Clemenceau, 20260 Calvi; Tel. 04 95 65 94 94; fax 04 95 65 29 71.* Set in the heart of the pleasure marina with rooms overlooking docked boats, the reception area of this hotel sits on traffic-free Rue Clemenceau just a few steps away from restaurants and shops. Rooms have A/C, TV, phone, mini-bar. Open all year. 37 rooms. Major credit cards.

Recommended Restaurants

Many restaurants are open in season only, usually from around April to October. Many also close one day per week, often on Monday. Lunch is generally served from noon to 2:30pm, dinner from 6pm. During the summer, resort restaurants may continue to serve until midnight; in the countryside they may not take in diners after 10pm.

All restaurants will have a *table d'hôte* or menu du jour (menu of the day), a three- or four-course lunch or dinner, which is always a good value. There may be several of these limited-choice menus at various price levels — the most expensive being the menu *gastronomique*. If you want to make the most of a tight budget, try the set lunch menu at a fine restaurant. Most restaurants will also offer *à la carte* (from the menu) service, but auberges (simple country restaurants) may only have a menu du jour.

You'll find that coastal restaurants sell seafood and country restaurants concentrate on meat dishes. Menus usually offer a mixture of French/Continental and Corsican dishes.

The French are generally heavy smokers and often there are few non-smoking tables available, but choosing a table out on the terrace rather than in the dining room usually solves this problem. Many restaurants accept dogs in the dining room.

Below is a selection of restaurants from each section of the guide. The accompanying price guides indicate average menu prices set per person at dinner without wine (which can add dramatically to the cost).

When calling any French telephone number from outside France, the initial 0 in the number is dropped: dial 00 33 4 and then the eight remaining numbers.

$$$$$	over 250F
$$$$	200–250F
$$$	140–200F
$$	100–140F
$	under 100F

THE SOUTHWEST

Auberge Santa Barbara $$–$$$ *Route de Propriano, Sartène Tel. 04 95 77 09 06.* A typical French provincial restaurant with understated yet competent service and wonderful food. Local and French dishes. Good value wine list. Garden dining in summer. Open mid-Mar to end of Sep. Dinner only 6pm–10:30pm. Major credit cards.

Chez Parenti $$$–$$$$ *Avenue Napoléon, Propriano; Tel. 04 95 76 12 14.* Overlooking the pleasure port, this family restaurant serves delicious seafood along with some meat and pasta dishes. They have a selection of local wines to accompany the menu. They also serve through the afternoon so you can eat when it suits you. Open 1 May–30 Sep daily 11am–10:30pm. Major credit cards.

Grand Café Napoléon $$$–$$$$ *10 cours Napoléon, Ajaccio; Tel. 04 95 21 42 54.* This is one of the oldest establishments in Ajaccio and a wonderful café for drinks. True French grand dining salon for dinner and a terrace for outside dining. Closed Sun and national holidays. Open dinner noon–2:30pm, dinner 6pm–10:30pm. Major credit cards.

Le 20123 $$$ *2, Rue Roi-de-Rome, Ajaccio; Tel. 04 95 21 50 05.* The family that owns this restaurant first ran one in a little inland village. They have attempted to bring the ambience of the village to this central Ajaccio site. Great country food and good atmosphere; it is very popular with local people. Closed 15 Jan–15 Feb, Sat mid-day and all day Mon. Lunch noon–2:30pm, dinner 6pm–10:30pm. Major credit cards.

Le Coralli $–$$ *Serragia (on the N overlooking Roccapina Bay); Tel. 04 95 77 05 94.* Wonderful views over the white sand bay of

Roccapina make this a great lunch stop. Simple menu of grilled meats and fish, salads, and local charcuterie. All these accompanied by local wine. Open daily noon–9:30pm. Major credit cards.

L'Hippocampe $$–$$$$$ *Rue Pandolphi, Propriano; Tel. 04 95 76 11 01.* Considered one of the best seafood restaurants on Corsica. Sit on the terrace under a vine canopy and enjoy the catch of the day or a plate of mixed seafood. *Oursins* (sea urchins) are a specialty for which Corsicans travel from miles around. Closed 1 Oct–1 Apr. Lunch noon–2:30pm, dinner 6pm–10:30pm. Major credit cards.

THE SOUTHEAST

Auberge du Col $$ *Col de Bavella; Tel. 04 95 57 43 87.* This rustic cabin-style restaurant sits just below the Col de Bavella on the forest side. They serve snacks and great charcuterie, but also make delicious pizzas cooked in a wood burning stove. A great place to rest after a hike in the woods. Closed 1 Nov–31 Mar. Open daily 11am–10:30pm. Major credit cards.

Bar L'Orriu $–$$ *5 Cours Napoléon, Porto-Vecchio; Tel. 04 95 70 26 21.* Not a restaurant in the true sense, but the few tables outside this delicatessen serve the best in local charcuterie and cheeses with platters of both, and delicious sandwiches. The great thing is that you can shop for whatever you like before you leave for a picnic. Closed mid-Feb to mid-Mar and Sun. Open 9am–12:30pm, 3pm–8pm (10:30pm in high season). Major credit cards.

L'Archivolto $$$ *Rue de l'Archivolto, the Citadel, Bonifacio; Tel. 04 95 73 17 58.* This small, unusual restaurant is set in a rustic stone building near the Sainte Marie-Majeure church. Its vaulted archways are filled with collectibles, old objects, and dressers full of old china. Outside is a small, sheltered terrace.

A limited menu of delicious meats and pasta, and an excellent ambience. Closed 1 Oct–31 Apr, lunchtime Sun. Open lunch noon–2:30pm, dinner 6:30pm–10:30pm. Major credit cards.

Le Tourisme $ *Cours Napoléon, Porto-Vecchio; Tel. 04 95 70 06 45.* A brasserie serving quick steak and fries but with a twist — try pasta with mint or local brocciu cheese. Exceptionally good value in one the most expensive resorts on the island. Open all year. Closed Sun lunch. Open noon–10:30pm, Sun 6pm–10:30pm.

Quatre Vents $$–$$$$ *29 Quai de Brando di Ferro, Bonifacio. Tel. 04 95 73 07 06.* Down along the harbor side, the Quatre Vents offers wonderful seafood in summer and menu items with meats typical of the local area all year round. Closed 15 Nov–5 Dec and 20 May–15 June. 15 Sep–30 June closed Mon. Open lunch noon–2:30pm, dinner 6pm–10:30pm. Major credit cards.

Sole e Monti $$$ *20122 Quenza; Tel. 04 95 78 62 53; fax 04 95 78 63 88.* Good local dishes at this small restaurant/hotel in Quenza. Well placed for touring the Col de Bavella and surrounding footpaths of the Alta Rocca. Local meats dishes and stews a specialty. Closed 1 Oct–1 May. Open daily lunch noon–1:45pm, dinner 7pm–8:45pm. Major credit cards.

Stella d'Oro $$$$ *7 rue Doria, Citadel, Bonifacio; Tel. 04 95 73 03 63.* Family owned restaurant with local clientele set in an old Bonifacio house. Rustic dishes of beef and lamb, along with seafood and fresh home-produced pasta. Closed 1 Nov–1 Mar. Open daily 11am–10:30pm. Major credit cards.

THE NORTHEAST AND CAP CORSE

A Casarella $$$$$ *Rue Saint-Croix, Le Citadel, Bastia; Tel. 04 95 32 02 32.* Beautiful views of the old port from this restaurant set in a narrow street in the citadel. It is well worth seeking out to experience the atmosphere of the citadel at night. Specialties include mussels and oysters from the nearby Etang du Bugiglia, and fresh meats from the interior of Corsica. Very popular with local people so it is always busy. Closed Nov, and Sun. Open lunch noon–2:30pm, dinner 6:30pm–10:30pm. Major credit cards.

Hôtel de la Corniche $$$–$$$$ *San-Martino-di-Lota, 20200 Bastia; Tel 04 95 31 40 98; fax 04 95 32 37 69.* Located 10 minutes' drive from Bastia in a hillside village, with wonderful views. This locally renowned restaurant uses the freshest local meats and seafood. French/Continental influences. Closed January. Open daily lunch noon–2:30pm, dinner 6:30pm–9:30pm. Major credit cards.

La Gaffe $$$–$$$$ *Port du St. Florent, St. Florent; Tel. 04 95 37 00 12.* Renowned seafood restaurant in the port with a loyal clientele. Langoustes (crayfish) are a specialty and are served in a variety of sauces. Extremely good selection of fresh fish to choose from. Closed 15 Nov–31 Jan. Closed Tues lunch. Major credit cards.

Le Plat d'Or $$$ *Place Paoli, Corte; Tel. 04 95 46 27 16.* Within view of the Paoli statue and with a little terrace, this restaurant works with the best farmers and food producers in the area to offer a menu of the land. Lamb and beef dishes are excellent; roast kid is occasionally on the menu. Fresh pasta and crepes are also available. Closed Christmas–1 Feb, and Sun.

Le Vieux Moulin $$–$$$$ *Le Port, 20238 Centuri; Tel. 04 95 35 60 15; fax 04 95 35 60 24.* Raised above the old port at Centuri, this fine 19th-century mansion with vine covered walls is a most impressive site. Beautiful terrace with views across the bay. Fresh seafood is a specialty but delicious meat dishes are also available. Open 1 Mar–31 Oct. Daily lunch noon–2:30pm, dinner 6:30pm–10:30pm. Major credit cards.

Le Zagora $$$ *4, Rue des Terrasses, Bastia; Tel. 04 95 34 12 01.* Small restaurant with views over the old port (enter one street behind the portside), which specializes in Moroccan dishes. Tender tagines (lamb stews) and cous-cous, along with grilled meats. Open all year. Closed Sun. Dinner only 6pm–11pm. Major credit cards.

U Sant'Agnellu $–$$ *20247 Rogliano; Tel. 04 95 35 40 59; fax 04 95 35 40 59.* A small family-owned rustic hotel restaurant at the very northern tip of Cap Corse. In the mountains, with views over the coastline and surrounding peaks. A simple but delicious menu taking the best seasonal ingredients, meats and seafood. Closed 1 Oct–1 Apr. Open daily lunch noon–2:30pm, dinner 6pm–9pm. Major credit cards.

THE NORTHWEST

A Pasturella $$$ *Monticello; Tel. 04 95 60 05 65.* Situated 4¹/2 km (2 miles) from l'Île-Rousse, this pretty restaurant serves a local menu with fresh seasonal ingredients. Specialty of roast kid, and seafood bought from the harbor every morning. Closed Nov and Sun evenings from Dec–31 Mar. Open lunch noon–2:30pm, dinner 6:30pm–11pm.

La Bergerie $$$$ *Route de Monticello l'Île-Rousse; Tel. 04 95 60 01 28.* Pretty converted farmhouse annexed to a hotel, with pleasant garden and Moorish/Mediterranean décor. Delicious menu of seafood and Continental dishes. Closed 1 Nov–1 Mar. Lunch noon–2:30pm, dinner 6pm–10:30pm. MasterCard and Visa.

La Villa $$$$$ *Chemin de Notre-Dame-de-la-Serra, 20260 Calvi; Tel. 04 95 65 10 10; web site <www.relaischateaux. fr/lavilla>* Beautiful views across Calvi Bay. The food is some of the finest on Corsica, accompanied by a splendid wine list. Continental cuisine using the freshest local ingredients. Closed 1 Jan–1 Apr. Open daily 11am–11pm. Major credit cards.

La Voute $$$ *Sant'Antonini; Tel. 04 95 61 74 71.* Set in an old olive mill dated 1893, at the edge of this pretty village in the Balagne, and with panoramic views of the surrounding country-side, La Voute makes a wonderful lunch stop. Local meat dishes a specialty. Closed 1 Oct–1 May. Open daily lunch noon–2:30pm, dinner 6pm–9pm. Major credit cards.

Le Mer $–$$ *Porto Marina, Porto; Tel. 04 95 26 11 27.* Set in the small bay with views of the sea and the castle, this restaurant has a terrace and a pretty dining room in a stone building. Seafood a specialty. Closed 16 Nov–14 Mar. Open daily lunch noon–2:30pm, dinner 6:30pm–10:30pm. Major credit cards.

Restaurant Santa Maria $–$$ *Place de l'Église, Calvi. Tel 04 95 65 04 19.* Set next to the square of Santa Maria church in the old town, this restaurant offers tables outside in the square or in an air-conditioned dining room. The daily specials are delicious and a very good value. Closed 1 Nov–1 Apr. Open daily lunch noon–2:30pm, dinner 6pm–10:30pm. Major credit cards.

U San Carlu $$$ *10 Place St. Charles, Calvi; Tel. 04 95 65 92 20.* Housed in the old city hospital, this Corsican family restaurant offers local cuisine. Views over the marina from the window tables. A range of fish, meats, charcuterie, and pasta dishes. Closed 1 Nov–1 Mar and Wed. Lunch noon–2:30pm, dinner 6:30pm–10:30pm. Major credit cards.

INDEX